Freedom from Sin's Dominion

SERIES EDITORS
Joel R. Beeke & Jay T. Collier

Interest in the Puritans continues to grow, but many people find the reading of these giants of the faith a bit unnerving. This series seeks to overcome that barrier by presenting Puritan books that are convenient in size and unintimidating in length. Each book is carefully edited with modern readers in mind, smoothing out difficult language of a bygone era while retaining the meaning of the original authors. Books for the series are thoughtfully selected to provide some of the best counsel on important subjects that people continue to wrestle with today.

Freedom from Sin's Dominion

John Owen

Edited by
Brian G. Hedges

Reformation Heritage Books
Grand Rapids, Michigan

Freedom from Sin's Dominion
© 2025 by Reformation Heritage Books

All rights reserved. No part of this book may be used or reproduced in any manner whatsoever without written permission except in the case of brief quotations embodied in critical articles and reviews. Direct your requests to the publisher at the following addresses:

Reformation Heritage Books
3070 29th St. SE
Grand Rapids, MI 49512
616-977-0889
orders@heritagebooks.org
www.heritagebooks.org

Originally published as *A Treatise of the Dominion of Sin and Grace* (London 1688)

Unless otherwise noted, quotations of Scripture are taken from the New King James Version®. Copyright © 1982 by Thomas Nelson. Used by permission. All rights reserved.

Scripture quotations marked KJV are taken from the King James Version. In the public domain.

Printed in the United States of America
25 26 27 28 29 30/10 9 8 7 6 5 4 3 2 1

Library of Congress Cataloging-in-Publication Data

Names: Owen, John, 1616-1683, author. | Hedges, Brian G., editor.
Title: Freedom from sin's dominion / John Owen ; edited by Brian G. Hedges.
Other titles: Treatise of the dominion of sin and grace
Description: Grand Rapids, Michigan : Reformation Heritage Books, [2025] | Series: Puritan treasures for today | Includes bibliographical references. | Summary: "An explanation of the way sin governs the human soul and how Christ overcomes that dominion and sets up His own reign in grace"—Provided by publisher.
Identifiers: LCCN 2025003516 (print) | LCCN 2025003517 (ebook) | ISBN 9798886861761 (paperback) | ISBN 9798886861778 (epub)
Subjects: LCSH: Sin—Christianity—Early works to 1800. | Christian life—Puritan authors.
Classification: LCC BT715 .O933 2025 (print) | LCC BT715 (ebook) | DDC 241/.3—dc23/eng/20250324
LC record available at https://lccn.loc.gov/2025003516
LC ebook record available at https://lccn.loc.gov/2025003517

Table of Contents

Preface... vii

1. Understanding the Dominion of Sin............. 1

Part 1: The Nature of Sin's Dominion

2. The Evil of Sin's Dominion..................... 11
3. Further Properties of Sin's Dominion........... 19

Part 2: The Signs of Sin's Dominion

4. The Difficulty of Discerning Sin's Dominion...... 33
5. Sin Possessing the Imagination 37
6. Dangerous Signs of Sin's Dominion 49
7. Graces and Duties for Mortifying Sin........... 57
8. Two Kinds of Hardness of Heart 71
9. Diagnosing the Dominion of Sin................. 77

**Part 3: The Assurance of Freedom
from Sin's Dominion**

10. Sin's Dominion over Those Under the Law 91
11. Grace Gives Strength Against Sin 99

12. Advice for Those Perplexed with Sin. 105
13. Freedom Through the Gospel. 111
14. The Mercy of Deliverance from Sin's Dominion. . . . 117
15. Be Sure You Are Not Under Sin's Dominion 127
16. Directions to Prevent Sin's Dominion. 133

Preface

Imagine the scenario. For several weeks you have felt an uncomfortable pain in your abdomen. You go to the doctor and undergo a series of tests, expecting nothing more than a mild prescription or a change in diet. A few days later, you are stunned to receive the diagnosis: stage 3 cancer.

You go to another doctor for a second opinion, and the diagnosis is confirmed. This is the bad news. The good news, you learn, is that the cancer is operable. And while the treatment will be both invasive and exhausting, the prognosis is hopeful. The regimen will be demanding—surgery, chemo, some significant lifestyle changes.

Though you experience some moments of anxiety, the dominant emotion is gratitude. You are grateful for your capable physician, the clear diagnosis, the referral to an expert oncologist, and a hopeful prognosis. You also have renewed feelings of gratitude for life itself, for God's providential mercies, and for caring family and friends. And you have a heightened sense of what's most important. Eternal things rest with greater weight on your soul.

This scenario is hypothetical for most. But it illustrates a spiritual parallel that is urgent for all. Sin is a spiritual cancer that leads to death apart from God's pardoning mercy and sanctifying grace.

We have all experienced its symptoms. And even Christians continue to wrestle with indwelling sin. These struggles often wreak havoc on Christian assurance. What we need is a capable physician of the soul who can diagnose our case and prescribe for us gospel medicine suited to restore us to spiritual health. John Owen (1616–1683) was just such a soul doctor.[1] And this book will help you with both diagnosis and cure.

Often called "the Prince of Puritans," Owen was one of the greatest theological minds of the whole Puritan era. But also, he had a pastor's heart. His writings merged theological precision and depth with pastoral sensitivity and devotional warmth in ways matched by few and surpassed by none.

Owen is perhaps best known for his famous trilogy on sin in which he treats the themes of mortification,

---

1. For a brief biography of Owen, see the entry in Joel Beeke and Randall J. Pederson, *Meet the Puritans: With a Guide to Modern Reprints* (Grand Rapids: Reformation Heritage Books, 2007), 455–63. For a full-length biography, see Crawford Gribben, *John Owen and English Puritanism: Experiences of Defeat* (Oxford: Oxford University Press, 2016).

temptation, and indwelling sin.[2] Each of these works were published within Owen's lifetime. But five years after his death, his widow published another book dealing with sin entitled *A Treatise of the Dominion of Sin and Grace*.[3] In this treatise, Owen expounded and applied the declaration of Romans 6:14: "For sin shall not have dominion over you, for you are not under law but under grace." The original subtitle reveals the scope of the book: "wherein sin's reign is discovered, in whom it is, and in whom it is not; how the law supports it; how grace delivers from it, by setting up its dominion in the heart."[4]

The book unfolds in three parts in which Owen examines first, the nature of sin's dominion; second, the evidence or signs of its dominion; and third, the grounds of assurance that believers are freed from sin's dominion, as expressed in Romans 6:14: "You are not under law but under grace."

---

2. The titles of the three books are *Of the Mortification of Sin in Believers*; *Of Temptation: The Nature and Power of It, Etc.*; and *The Nature, Power, Deceit and Prevalency of the Remainders of Indwelling Sin in Believers*, all in volume 6 of *The Works of John Owen*, ed. W. H. Goold (1850–1853: repr., Edinburgh: Banner of Truth, 1966). The trilogy has more recently been published as one volume entitled *Overcoming Sin and Temptation*, ed. Justin Taylor and Kelly M. Kapic (Wheaton, Ill.: Crossway, 2006).

3. This is found in Owen, *Works*, 7:499–560.

4. Owen, *Dominion of Sin and Grace*, in *Works*, 7:499.

At the heart of the treatise is Owen's careful analysis (in part 2) of certain symptoms or signs that might be taken as solid evidence that, on one hand, someone is free from sin's reign when, in fact, they are not; or, on the other, that they are under the thralldom of sin (and thus unregenerate) when, in fact, grace may reign in their hearts. Owen's method of sifting through these various signs and symptoms and distinguishing those that point to sin's dominion from those that do not, reveal (to use the words of W. H. Goold) "all his singular powers of spiritual analysis."[5]

Genuine believers who are deeply engaged in conflict with sin will here find in these pages both the consolation of the gospel and wise directions for fighting the good fight of faith. So-called carnal Christians, who may, in fact, be unbelievers, may by God's grace find this book to be a means of spiritual awakening as they honestly confront their spiritual bondage, and then conversion, as they follow Dr. Owen's prescription for seeking salvation through faith in the crucified Christ.

When the nineteenth-century Scottish professor John Duncan assigned Owen's book on indwelling sin to his students, he added the warning, "Gentlemen, prepare yourselves for the knife!"[6] The same could be said of this

---

[5]. Owen, *Dominion of Sin and Grace*, in *Works*, 7:500.

[6]. As told by J. I. Packer, *A Quest for Godliness: The Puritan Vision of the Christian Life* (Wheaton, Ill.: Crossway, 2010), 194.

book, for those who read it attentively will certainly experience the surgeon's scalpel.

But this book does more than wound. It also heals. For Owen both applies the sharp two-edged scalpel of the word *and* ministers the soothing balm of the gospel to our hearts. The remedy of grace becomes especially clear in part 3, where Owen expounds on the ground of our assurance as believers that sin will not reign over us, as found in Paul's words: "You are not under law but under grace." In drawing out the implied contrast between law and grace, Owen shows that in the gospel God has done what the law could never do. He has set us free from sin:

> For what the law could not do in that it was weak through the flesh, God did by sending His own Son in the likeness of sinful flesh, on account of sin: He condemned sin in the flesh, that the righteous requirement of the law might be fulfilled in us who do not walk according to the flesh but according to the Spirit. (Rom. 8:3–4)

This edition of Owen's book, retitled *Freedom from Sin's Dominion*, has been modernized for today's readers. Archaic terms have been replaced with more familiar words, Latin quotations have been replaced with English translations, and lengthy chapters have been broken down into shorter, more manageable sections. Owen's long, meandering sentences have been broken down into shorter, simpler ones. Finally, the overall structure and development of Owen's argument has been clarified with a simpler outline and the addition of subheadings.

I encourage you to read this book prayerfully, asking the Lord to search and try your heart. Use the prayer of Psalm 139:23–24 (KJV): "Search me, O God, and know my heart: try me, and know my thoughts: and see if there be any wicked way in me, and lead me in the way everlasting."

CHAPTER 1

Understanding the Dominion of Sin

Dealing with God in prayer about sin, the psalmist acknowledges that in all men there are unsearchable errors of life, beyond all human understanding or comprehension, along with such daily sins of infirmity as stand in need of continual cleansing and pardon. "Who can understand his errors? Cleanse me from secret faults" (Ps. 19:12). And yet he supposes that these things are consistent with a state of grace and acceptance with God. He had no thought of any absolute perfection in this life or of any such condition that would no longer need continual cleansing and pardon. In light of this, therefore, we can say that there are (or may be) such sins in believers (yes, many of them) that yet, under a due application to God for purifying and pardoning grace, will neither deprive us of peace here nor endanger our salvation hereafter.

But the psalmist then speaks of another sort of sins, which, partly from their nature (what they are in themselves) and partly from their operation and power, will certainly prove destructive to men's souls wherever they are.

> Keep back Your servant also
>   from presumptuous sins;
> Let them not have dominion over me.
> Then I shall be blameless,
> And I shall be innocent of great transgression.
>   (Ps. 19:13)

This is the hinge on which the whole cause and state of my soul turns: Although I am subject to many sins of various sorts, yet under them all I can and do maintain my integrity and covenant uprightness in walking with God. And where I fail, I am kept within the reach of cleansing and pardoning mercy, which is continually administered to my soul by Jesus Christ. But there is a state of life in this world in which the soul, under sin's dominion, acts with presumption and is inconsistent with integrity and freedom from condemning guilt. Therefore, he earnestly condemns this state, which alone ruins men's souls for eternity, and prays to be kept and preserved from it.

What the psalmist so earnestly prays for, the apostle Paul, in the words of Romans 6:14, promises to all believers by virtue of the grace of Christ Jesus administered in the gospel. Both the prayer of the prophet for himself and the promise of the apostle in the name of God to us manifest how great the importance of this matter is, as I will declare it to be immediately.

There are several things supposed or included in these words of the apostle that we must first examine.

Without these, we will not rightly understand the truth proposed in his words.

The Reality of Indwelling Sin

It is supposed that sin still abides in and dwells with believers. For this is the implication of the words, the sin that is in you "shall not have dominion over you" (Rom. 6:14). In other words, the apostle speaks of believers, not those who are insensitive to sin or who do not groan to be delivered from it as the apostle does (Rom. 7:24). Such people know neither themselves nor what sin or the grace the gospel consists of. There is the "flesh" remaining in everyone, which "lusts against the Spirit" (Gal. 5:17), and it adheres to all the faculties of our souls. Thus, it is called the "old man" (Rom. 6:6), in contrast to the renovation of our minds and their faculties, which are called the "new man" (Eph. 4:24), or new creature, in us. And there is a continual "provision for the flesh, to fulfill its lusts" (Rom. 13:14). So the flesh abides in us in the way of a dying, decaying habit that is weakened and impaired; but it acts itself in inclinations, motions, and desires that are suitable to its nature.

As Scripture and experience concur in teaching this, so a supposition of it is the only ground of the whole doctrine of evangelical mortification. This is a duty that is incumbent on believers all the days of their lives. Without this, believers can never perform any other duty in an appropriate manner. No one will deny this except those who are wholly under the power of atheistic blindness or, through the fever of spiritual pride, have lost the understanding of their own miserable condition and so lie dreaming about absolute perfection. But we're not now concerned with these sorts of people.

The first proper object of this mortification is the sin that dwells within us. This is the "flesh," which is to be "mortified," and the "old man," which is to be "crucified." These are the "passions and desires" of the flesh, which, with all their corrupt inclinations, actings, and motions, are to be destroyed (Gal. 5:24; see Rom. 6:6; Col. 3:5). Unless this is well fixed in our minds, we cannot understand the greatness of the grace and privilege expressed here in the apostle's words.

The Power of Indwelling Sin

It is supposed that this sin, which remains and dwells in believers to various degrees, may exercise its power in them with the intent of gaining victory and dominion over them. It is first supposed that sin has this dominion in some people, ruling over all unbelievers (all who are under the law), and then that sin will attempt to do the same in those who believe and are under grace. For in the affirmation that sin will not have dominion over us, Paul grants that it contends for dominion but says that it will not have success or prevail. That is why Scripture says that sin fights within us (Rom. 7:23) and wars against our souls (1 Peter 2:11). And the reason it fights within us is to obtain dominion, for that is the purpose of all war. Whatever fights does so in order to gain power and rule.

This, then, is the general aim of sin in all its operations. Its work varies according to the variety of lusts in the minds of men. But its general aim in them all is to have dominion. Where anyone is tempted and seduced by his own lust, as the apostle James says, even if it is a small temptation or so unusual as to never occur again, the design of sin lies not in the temptation itself but rather to use it as a means to gain dominion over the soul. This consideration should keep believers always on guard against the motions of sin, even if they seem like small sins or their occasions are unlikely to return. For the aim and tendency of each one is dominion and death. If sin is not stopped in its progress, this is where sin leads, as the apostle James declares (James 1:14–15). Therefore, do not believe its flatteries: "Isn't it only a little one?" "This is the first time." "This will be the last time." "This takes only a small part of my mind and heart." "It will not go further than this." Do not allow any room for the urgency and solicitations of sin. Do not consider any of its excuses or promises, for its one aim is to gain power over your souls and bring them to ruin.

Sin Works by Deceit and Force

There are two general ways by which sin exercises its power and aims at obtaining dominion. These are the only two ways by which anyone can design or attain an unjust dominion. These ways are *deceit* and *force*. I have fully described both of these in another book.[1] In regard to both, it is promised to the poor and needy that the Lord Christ shall "redeem their soul from deceit and violence" (Ps. 72:12–14 KJV).

These are the only two ways of obtaining an unjust dominion. And where they are joined together, they will have mighty power, which will make the contest hazardous. There are few believers who have not found it so, at least in their own thoughts. At one time or another, they have been ready to say, "We will one day fall by the hand of this enemy" and have been forced to cry out to Jesus Christ for help and support with the same intensity the disciples felt at sea when the ship was covered with waves and they cried, "Lord, save us! We are perishing!" (Matt. 8:24–25). And they would have perished, had the Lord not quickly come to their aid (Heb. 2:18). The soul frequently experiences the power of Christ's grace just as the disciples upon their outcry experienced His sovereign authority, when He "rebuked the winds and the sea, and there was a great calm" (Matt. 8:26).

It is this dominion of sin against which we are given security. Though sin abides in us and contends for rule by deceit and force, it will not prevail. It will not have dominion.

---

1. See John Owen, *Indwelling Sin in Believers* (Edinburgh: Banner of Truth, 2010).

Understanding the Dominion of Sin

This is very important to us. Our souls are necessarily under the rule of some principle or law. And our spiritual state is determined by this rule. We are either the slaves "of sin leading to death, or of obedience leading to righteousness" (Rom. 6:16). The substance of the apostle's teaching in Romans 6 is that the state of the soul leading to either eternal life or death follows the conduct and rule that we are under. If sin has dominion, we are lost forever. If it is dethroned, we are safe. It may tempt, seduce, and entice. It may fight, war, perplex, and disquiet. It may surprise us into actual sin. Yet if sin does not have dominion in us, we are in a state of grace and acceptance with God.

The Structure of the Argument of This Book

I will consider three things from the words of Romans 6:14, "Sin shall not have dominion over you, for you are not under law but under grace":

1. The nature of sin's dominion: What is that dominion of sin from which we are freed by grace?

2. The signs of sin's dominion: How may we know whether sin has dominion in us or not?

3. The assurance of freedom from sin's dominion: What is the reason for the assurance here given to us that sin will not have dominion over us—namely, because we are "not under law but under grace"?

PART 1

The Nature of Sin's Dominion

*What is that dominion of sin
from which we are freed by grace?*

CHAPTER 2

The Evil of Sin's Dominion

What is the dominion of sin that we are freed from and discharged of by grace? To answer this, I will describe some properties of sin's dominion that will reveal its general nature. After this, I will consider the particulars in which this dominion consists.

The dominion of sin is perverse and evil for two reasons, the same two reasons that make any rule or dominion to be evil: because it is usurped and destructive.

Usurped Dominion

Sin has no right to rule in the souls of men. Men have no power to give sin a right to rule over them. They may voluntarily enslave themselves to sin, but this does not give sin the right or authority to rule. From their origin, all men have another Lord to whom they owe all obedience—namely, God. Nothing can discharge them from their duty to this obligation to God and His law. As the apostle says, "Do you not know that to whom you present yourselves slaves to obey, you are that one's slaves whom you obey, whether of sin leading to death, or of obedience leading to righteousness?" (Rom. 6:16). And so it is. By their own voluntary subjection to sin, men become the servants of sin. But this does not give sin authority over and against the law of God, which has the sole right to rule in the souls of men. For all who give themselves up to the service of sin are living in actual rebellion against their true Lord.

Several things follow from this. First, it shows the great aggravation of the evil of being in a state of sin. Men who live in sin voluntarily wrest themselves from under the rule of God's law and give themselves to be slaves to this tyrant, sin. If sin could lay any claim to this dominion or had some title to plead, it would partly alleviate the guilt of those who give themselves up to sin. But, as the apostle says, men "yield" themselves (Rom. 6:16 KJV) to the slavery of sin. They reject the rule of God's law and choose this foreign yoke. This only aggravates their sin and misery. And yet the vast majority of people visibly and openly show themselves to be the servants of sin. They wear its uniform and do its work. They boast in their bondage and never think themselves so courageous as when, by profane swearing, drunkenness, uncleanness, covetousness, and scoffing at religion, they openly avow the lord whom they serve, the master to whom they do belong. But whatever they may dream in the meantime, their "destruction does not slumber" (2 Peter 2:3).

The Evil of Sin's Dominion

From this it also follows that all people have an inherent right to cast off the rule of sin and vindicate themselves into liberty. If they only will, they might plead the right and title of God's law to rule over their souls to the utter exclusion of all the pleas and pretenses of sin for power. They have the right to say to sin, "Get away!" "What have I to do anymore with idols?" (Isa. 30:22; Hos. 14:8).

All people, I say, have this right in themselves because of the allegiance they naturally owe to God's law. But they do not have the power in themselves to execute this right and actually cast off the yoke of sin. This is the work of grace. Sin's dominion is broken only by grace.

But you will say then, "To what end does this right serve, if people have no power in themselves to put it in execution? And how can it be charged as an aggravation of their sin that they do not use this right, seeing they have no power so to do? Will you blame someone who had a right to an estate for not claiming it when he had no means to do so?" I will briefly offer three answers.

First, no living man neglects the use of this right to cast off the yoke and dominion of sin because he *cannot* make use of it but merely because he *will not*. He voluntarily chooses to continue living under the power of sin and looks on everything that would deliver him as an enemy. "Because the carnal mind is enmity against God; for it is not subject to the law of God, nor indeed can be" (Rom. 8:7). Any time the law comes to claim its right and rule over the soul, the man under sin's power considers the law as his enemy coming to disturb his peace. He fortifies his mind against the law. And when the gospel comes and offers the way and means for the soul's deliverance, offering both aid and assistance to that end, this also is considered as an enemy. Thus, the gospel and all its offers are rejected (see Prov. 1:24–31; John 3:19). This, then, is the condition of everyone who abides under the dominion of sin: *he chooses to do so*. He continues in this state by an act of his own will. He avows enmity against everything that would give him deliverance. This will be a painful aggravation of his condemnation on the last day.

Second, God may justly require that anyone who is under the power of the grace of the gospel should cast off sin's dominion. For this is daily proposed to them in the preaching of the gospel, and the gospel enables them to do so. And though we do not know the ways and means of the effectual communication of grace to men's souls, yet this is certain: that grace is so offered in the preaching of the gospel that no one will go without grace or be destitute of its aid and assistance, except those who willfully chose to refuse and reject it. This is what the whole cause depends on. "But you are not willing to come to Me that you may have life" (John 5:40), and this all unbelievers have (or may have) the experience of in themselves. If they duly examine themselves, they should know they have voluntarily refused the assistance of the grace that is offered for their deliverance. Therefore, they destroy themselves.

The Evil of Sin's Dominion

But third, there is a time when men also lose even the right. The bond servants in the Old Testament who gave up themselves to have their ears bored lost all claims to freedom; they were not even liberated in the Year of Jubilee. Similarly, there is a time when God judicially gives men up to the rule of sin to forever live under its power, so that they lose all right to freedom. God dealt this way with many of the idolatrous Gentiles of old (Rom. 1:24, 26, 28), and so He continues to deal with similarly profligate sinners. He acts in this way toward many in the anti-Christian world (2 Thess. 2:11–12) and with many who despise the gospel (Isa. 6:9–10). When it comes to this, the case is decided, and such men lose even the right and title to be free from the dominion of sin.

They may sometimes fret in the painful feelings of shame that pursue many in their uncleanness in the slavery to sin. But if God has judicially given them over to sin, they no longer have even the right to pray for deliverance. Nor will they do so, for they are bound in the fetters of cursed presumption or despair. Observe their work and wages (Rom. 2:5–6). This is the most woeful state and condition of sinners in this world. It is an unavoidable entrance into the chambers of death.

If you have lived for a long time under the power of sin, beware lest what is spoken of in these scriptures comes upon you! But if you will now put your claim in the court of heaven, you yet have a right to be delivered from your bondage and servitude. But you do not know how soon you may be deprived of this by God judicially giving you up to sin and Satan. Then all complaints will be too late, and all the springs of endeavor for relief will be completely dried up. All your reserves for a future repentance will be cut off, and all your cries will be despised (Prov. 1:24–31). Therefore, while it is yet called today, harden not your hearts, lest God swear in His wrath that you shall never enter into His rest (see Ps. 95:7–11; Heb. 3:7–10).

In order that you may be warned, take note of the signs, or symptoms, of the approach of such an irrecoverable condition. These symptoms are the following:

- A long continuance in the practice of any known sin. There are limits to divine patience. The longsuffering of God waits for repentance for a time (1 Peter 3:20; 2 Peter 3:9). But there is a time when His patience endures only "with much longsuffering the vessels of wrath prepared for destruction" (Rom. 9:22). This is commonly after a long continuance in known sin.

- When convictions have been digested and warnings have been despised. God does not usually deal in this way with men until they have rejected the means of their deliverance. There is a generation, indeed, who, from their youth live in contempt of God. The psalmist describes such proud sinners (e.g., Ps. 10:2–7).

The Evil of Sin's Dominion

There are seldom any indications of the execution of the decree against these sorts of men. The evidence of it is their "add[ing] drunkenness to thirst" (Deut. 29:19 KJV), one kind of sin to another, of making a visible progress in sinning, of adding boasting and profane contempt of all things sacred to their course in sin. But ordinarily those who are in danger of this judicial hardness have had warnings and convictions. These made some impression on them. But now they are left without any calls and rebukes, or at least without any sense of them.

+ When men contract the guilt of such sins as seem to establish them in the unpardonable sin against the Holy Ghost, such as proud, contemptuous, malicious reproaches of the ways of God; of holiness; of the Spirit of Christ and His gospel. These sorts of people are frequently marked in Scripture as those who are at least near to a final and fatal rejection.

+ A voluntary renunciation of the means of grace and of their professed conversion to God that men have enjoyed. This is commonly accompanied by hatred of the word and those ministers by whom it is dispensed. Such persons God frequently (and visibly) irrecoverably gives over to the dominion of sin. He declares that He will have nothing more to do with them.

- The resolved choice of wicked, profane, unclean, and scoffing society. It is very rare that any are recovered from this snare. And there are many other signs of the near approach of such a hardening judgment that will give up men everlastingly to the service of sin. O that poor sinners would wake up before it is too late!

Destructive Dominion

The dominion of sin is evil and perverse not only because it is unjust and usurped but also because it is always used and exercised to destructive ends, to the hurt and ruin of its subjects. A tyrant, or usurper, may make use of his power and rule for good ends, for the good of those over whom he rules. But all the ends of the dominion of sin are evil to sinners. Sin in its rule will pretend fair and offer various advantages and satisfactions to their minds. They will have wages for their work; pleasure and profit will come in by it. Indeed, on various pretenses, sin will promise them eternal rest when all is finished—or, at least, that they will not fail to obtain rest by anything they do in sin's service. And by such means sin keeps them secure under its dominion. But sin's true design is the eternal ruin of the souls of all who are under its power. But sinners will understand this only when it is too late (Jer. 2:13, 19).

CHAPTER 3

Further Properties of Sin's Dominion

In this chapter we will consider several further properties of sin's dominion.

Forceful Dominion

Sin's dominion has the force and power of a law in the minds and wills of its subjects. This dominion of sin is not a mere force against the will and endeavors of those under it. There is no dominion when sin's power and interest consist only in putting a force on the mind and soul by its temptations. Sin may perplex these people, but it does not rule over them. But where sin has dominion, it has the force and power of a law in the wills and minds of its subjects. By this, sin requires their obedience, and they present themselves to obey it as its slaves (Rom. 6:16).

This is why some degree of the will's consent is a part of sin's dominion. The will's steadfast reluctance to sin and its conquering force against sin defeats sin's title to rule and hold dominion. The apostle fully declares this in the next chapter, Romans 7. The will is the ruling faculty and power of the soul. The principle that acts within it and determines it has the rule. Notwithstanding light and conviction, the determination of the whole soul toward either duty or sin is found in the power of the will. If the will to sin is taken away, sin cannot have dominion.

Here is wisdom: Whoever can distinguish between the impressions of sin *upon* him and the rule of sin *in* him is in the way of peace. But this is often not easy to discern, as we will further see, along with the reasons for this difficulty. On the one hand, by their unavoidable impressions on the will, convictions will make a great pretense and appearance of opposition to sin—even when the will itself is not actually opposed to sin. And on the other hand, disturbed affections under temptations will plead that the will itself is given up to the choice and service of sin, even when it is not so. The will in this matter is like the Theban's shield: so long as it was safe, they imagined themselves victorious even in death.[1] But this case is determined by the light of Scripture and experience, which is what this treatise seeks to clarify.

Exclusive Dominion

Sin's dominion cannot coexist with the rule of God's

---

1. This is a reference to the death of Epaminodas, the general of Thebes, who defeated the Spartans in the Theban war in the fourth century BC. When Epaminodas was dying at Mantinea, he asked if his shield was safe.

Further Properties of Sin's Dominion

Spirit and grace. The Spirit has the sovereign rule in all believers. They are led by the Spirit, guided by the Spirit, acted on and ruled by Him, and thus are under the government of God and Christ, and no other.

But the rule of sin is absolutely inconsistent with this. No one can serve these two masters at the same time. Grace and sin may be in the same soul at the same time, but they cannot bear rule in the same soul at the same time. There is only one throne in the soul, and it will admit only one ruler. Every evidence we have of being under the rule of grace is so that we are not under the dominion of sin.

Therefore, this is the primary way to secure our peace and comfort against the pretenses of sin resulting in the distress of our consciences. Let us strive to preserve an experience of the rule of grace in our hearts (Col. 3:15). We are under the conduct and rule of either sin or grace. There is no combination of these two, no partnership between them in their rule. They may share residence in the soul, but not the rule. If we can assure ourselves of being under the rule of one, we secure ourselves against the other. It is therefore our wisdom to obtain experience and evidence of being under the rule of grace. This lies at the foundation of all our comforts. If grace rules, it will show itself—as long as we observe its motions and operations within us.

And grace will show itself in two ways. First, it shows itself by maintaining a constant purpose in living for God and in conformity to Christ, in spite of the surprise attacks of temptation and the most urgent solicitations of sin. This purpose is called continuing with the Lord "with purpose of heart" (Acts 11:23). Wherever grace has the rule, this will be present.

It is like a man going to sea who purposes to go to a certain place and port and so plots his course. On his journey he may meet with storms and crosswinds that drive him off course and sometimes directly backward toward where he started. But his purpose still holds. And in pursuit of this purpose, he applies his skill and hard work to recover all the losses caused by the storms and crosswinds that drove him back.

So it is with a soul under the conduct of grace. Its fixed design is to live to God, but in its course, it meets with the storms and crosswinds of temptation and various strategies of sin. These disturb him, disorder him, and sometimes drive him backward, as if he would take a contrary course and return to the coast of sin from which he had set out. But where grace has the rule and conduct, it will weather all these oppositions and obstructions. It will restore the soul, bring it again into order, and recover it from the confusions and evil dispositions into which it has been drawn. It will give a fresh strength to its chief design of living for God in all things. It will do this constantly, as often as the soul meets with such disturbances from the power of sin. When there is a deeply rooted firmness and strength in purpose, it will work itself out through all changes and variations. But when the strength of any cause is temporary, the first opposition and disorder will ruin us. So if men's purpose in living for God is only temporary, resulting from present convictions, then the first vigorous opposition or temptation will overthrow it. But where there is this rooted design of the soul springing from the power of grace, it will break through all such oppositions and recover its power in the mind and affections. By this it shows its rule and that the whole interest of sin in the soul is by rebellion and not by virtue of dominion.

Second, the soul under the rule of grace will maintain the constant exercise of grace in all religious duties, or at least a sincere effort to do so.[2] Where sin has dominion, it can allow the soul to perform religious duties—indeed, in some cases to abound in them. But it will take care that

---

2. By "exercise of grace," Owen has in mind the active engagement of the graces, or virtues, of the renewed heart, such as faith, hope, and love. As Owen said in one of his sermons,

> God makes room, as it were, in his vineyard for the budding, flourishing, and fruit-bearing of other plants which he hath planted. Great employments call for great exercise of graces. Even in employments in and about providential things, there is the exercise of spiritual grace—as much faith and prayer, as much communion with God, walking before him, and wrestling with him, may be used in casting down of armies, as in setting up of churches. God exerciseth all the graces of his in the work he calleth them out unto.

Sermon 8: "The Labouring Saint's Dismission to Rest," in *Works*, 8:354.

divine grace is not exercised in them. There may be some delight in duties or other motions of affection caused by light, gifts, afflictions, or superstition. But there will be no exercises of faith or love in them, for these belong essentially and inseparably to the rule of grace. And where grace has the controlling influence, the soul will endeavor to maintain the constant exercise of grace in all its duties and will never be satisfied in them without some sense of grace. Where it fails in this, it will judge itself and watch against similar attacks. Indeed, except in the case of great temptation, the present sense of sin's guilt, which is the highest obstruction to the spiritual boldness required in the due exercise of grace (that is, faith and love in holy duties), will not hinder the soul from striving after grace and its use.

Through these means and similar inseparable operations of grace we can have an assuring experience that under the rule and conduct of grace, we may be free in our minds from disturbing and anxious thoughts that sin has dominion over us. For sin and grace cannot both bear sway in the same soul.

Conscious Dominion

For sin to hold dominion, it is required that it make the soul conscious of its power and rule. Or at least sin operates in ways that will make a person conscious of its work, unless their conscience is so completely seared and hardened as to be "past feeling" (Eph. 4:19). For there is no rule or dominion unless those subjected to it are (or at least may be) conscious of it.

Further Properties of Sin's Dominion

Repressing the Convictions of the Mind

There are two ways in which sin in its dominion will make its subjects conscious of its rule. First, sin will make those in whom it has dominion conscious of its power in repressing and overcoming the efficacy of the convictions of the mind. Those who are under the dominion of sin may have light into and conviction of their duty in many things. And they might ordinarily follow this light and conviction, notwithstanding the dominion of sin. A tyrant will permit his slaves and subjects to ordinarily follow their own causes. But if what they would do (either in matter or manner) begins to interfere with or oppose his interests, he will make them conscious of his power.

In the same way, if men have light and conviction where sin has dominion, it will allow them ordinarily, and in many ways, to comply with the light. It will allow them to pray, to hear the word, to abstain from various sins, and to perform many duties. This is clearly affirmed in the Scriptures of many who were under the power of sin, and we see it in experience. How much work do we see about religion and religious duties, what constant observation of religious times and seasons, and how many duties that in themselves are morally good and useful are done by those who on many other accounts show themselves to be under the dominion of sin! But if the light and conviction of such people begin to rise in opposition to the principal interest of sin in those lusts and ways in which it exercises its rule, it will make conscious of its power. In those who stifle or shut their eyes or cast out of the mind or go directly contrary to their convictions, light will first show discontent, then seek relief through resolutions to change in other times and seasons. But sin, by virtue of its dominion, will carry the cause.

Two things follow from this. First, a constant dislike for sin, arising from light in the mind and conviction in the conscience, does not prove that someone is not under sin's dominion. For until blindness and hardness completely overtake men, there is within them a discerning between good and evil, along with self-judging thoughts, as the apostle declares: They "show the work of the law written in their hearts, their conscience also bearing witness, and between themselves their thoughts accusing or else excusing them" (Rom. 2:15). And in this many people satisfy themselves. When their light condemns sin, they suppose that they hate it. But they do not. When convictions call for duties, they suppose that they love them. But they do not. What they look on as the rule of light within them in opposition to sin is just the rebellion of a natural enlightened conscience against the dominion of sin in the heart. In other words, the light of conscience can condemn every known sin, keep someone from committing many sins, press for obedience to every known duty, and lead to the performance of many duties, while sin still has full dominion in the soul. And it will show itself when it comes to the test in those instances where it exercises its ruling power.

Further Properties of Sin's Dominion

The second thing is that those whose minds are continually caught between the conduct of their light and the urgency of conviction, on one hand, and the rule or dominion of sin, on the other, are in a miserable condition. Light, wherever it is, has the right to rule. This is the art by which the mind leads itself. And for men to be forced by the power of their lusts to act often against their light is a sad and deplorable condition. Such it is with those over whom sin has dominion. Such persons are said to "rebel against the light" (Job 24:13) because of its right to rule in them, where it is deposed by sin. This makes most men like "the troubled sea, when it cannot rest, whose waters cast up mire and dirt" (Isa. 57:20).

Continual Solicitation of the Mind

Second, sin will also make those in whom it has dominion conscious of its power by its continual solicitation of the mind and affections with respect to the sin (or numerous sins) in which it primarily exercises its rule. Having possessed the will and inclinations of the mind with the affections, as it does wherever its dominion is absolute, sin continually disposes, inclines, and stirs up the mind toward those sins. It will level the bent of the whole soul toward such sins or the circumstances of them. There is no more pregnant discovery of sin's rule in anyone than this, that it habitually engages the mind and affections to be constantly preoccupied with some sin or another.

And yet, notwithstanding these indications of sin's ruling power, I must add that there are few in whom sin has dominion who are convinced of their state and condition. Many are so under the power of darkness, of inactive sloth and negligence, and are so desperately wicked that they have no consciousness of this rule of sin. Such are those described by the apostle in Ephesians 4:18–19: "Having their understanding darkened, being alienated from the life of God, because of the ignorance that is in them, because of the blindness of their heart; who, being past feeling, have given themselves over to lewdness, to work all uncleanness with greediness."

And though they are the vilest slaves who live on earth, they judge no one to be free but themselves. They look on others as being in bondage to foolish and superstitious fears while they are free to drink, swear, scoff at religion, whore, and defile themselves without restraint. This is their liberty, and they have what is as good as in hell—liberty to curse and blaspheme God and to run with vengeful thoughts on themselves and the whole creation. The light in such people is darkness itself, in that there is nothing within them to rise in opposition to the rule of sin. With this missing, they have no way of sensing sin's power within. Others, as we have already observed, while living in some compliance with their light and convictions and abstaining from many sins and performing many duties, yet live in known sin and allow themselves in it, but will not acknowledge that sin has dominion in them.

From this we see there are two difficult things in this case:

Further Properties of Sin's Dominion

First, it is difficult to convince those in whom sin obviously has dominion that they are really slaves of sin. For they do their best to keep away such convictions. Some justify themselves; some excuse themselves and do not even consider this matter. It is a rare thing, especially now, for anyone to be brought under this conviction by the preaching of the word, though there are multitudes who hear it.

Second, it is difficult to convince others that sin does *not* have dominion—in spite of sin's restless motions in them and warring against their souls.

Yet unless this can be done, it is impossible for them to enjoy solid peace and comfort in this life. This is the great concern of the best believers, so long as they live in this world. For as they grow in light, spirituality, experience, freedom of mind, and humility, the more they will desire to know also the deceit, activity, and power of remaining sin in their hearts.

And although sin does not work in them (at least not consciously) toward those sins by which it reigns and rages in others, yet they are able to discern its more subtle, inward, and spiritual acts in the mind and heart which leads to the weakening of grace, the obstruction of its effectual operations in holy duties, along with the many disinclinations to stability in the life of God. And this fills their souls with trouble.

PART 2

The Signs of Sin's Dominion

How may we know whether sin has dominion in us or not?

CHAPTER 4

The Difficulty of Discerning Sin's Dominion

Having considered the nature of sin's dominion, we can now move forward to our principal concern—namely, how to discern whether or not we are under sin's dominion and, thus, whether we are under the law or under grace and what is the state of our souls in relation to God. This is a very needful question for some to ask. Everyone needs to have this rightly settled in their minds from Scripture and experience, for all our solid peace hangs on this. Sin is going to be within us—it will lust, fight, and entice us. But, when it comes to our peace and comfort, the great question is this: Does sin have dominion over us or not?

Our concern here is not with those in whom the reign of sin is absolute and easily discerned (if not to themselves yet to others). There are those who visibly present their members "as instruments of unrighteousness to sin" (Rom. 6:13). Sin reigns in their mortal bodies, and they openly "obey it in its lusts" (v. 12). They are openly slaves "of sin leading to death" (v. 16) and are not ashamed of it.

> The look on their countenance witnesses
> against them,
> And they declare their sin as Sodom;
> They do not hide it. (Isa. 3:9)

Such are those described in Ephesians 4:18–19, and this world is filled with such people. These are those people who are under the power of darkness and enmity against God and act in the service of various lusts in opposition to all serious godliness. There is no question concerning their state. They themselves cannot deny that it is so. I say these things not to give liberty for censuring others but for clarity in discernment. Those who openly wear sin's uniform may well be considered sin's servants—and they shall not fail to receive sin's wages. Though they may now be conceited and despise all manner of convictions, at the end they will find it bitter (Isa. 50:11; Eccl. 11:9).

There are many, however, in whom the case is uncertain and not easily determined. For, on one hand, they may have various things in them that seem opposed to the reign of sin yet are not really inconsistent with it. All their arguments and pleas for vindication may fail them when tried. On the other hand, there may be some in whom the powerful workings of sin are so great and perplexing as to argue that sin has dominion, when it is actually only a stubborn rebel.

There are five things which seem destructive to and inconsistent with the dominion of sin but actually are not.

Illumination

This includes knowledge and spiritual gifts, convictions about good and evil and about all known duties and sins. Some people have this and yet live in perpetual rebellion against it in some way or another.

Changed Affections

Another uncertain sign is a change in the affections that brings temporary delight in religious duties, along with some consistency in observing them. But this is also found in many who are yet evidently under the power of sin and spiritual darkness.

Performance of Duties

The performance of many moral or evangelical duties or the conscientious abstinence from many sins is another uncertain sign. We see this with the rich young man who was yet lacking what was needful to free him from the dominion of sin (Matt. 19:20–23).

Legal or Partial Repentance

Many assure themselves by their repentance. And when repentance is gracious, evangelical, a fruit of faith, and consists of the return of the whole soul to God, it is a blessed security. But there is a kind of repentance that is legal, partial, and concerns only particular sins. And this kind of repentance is not pleadable[1] in this case. Ahab was no less under sin's dominion after he repented than he was before, and Judas repented before hanging himself (see 1 Kings 21–22; Matt. 27:3–5).

Promises and Resolutions

Many make promises and resolutions against committing sin in the future. But as the prophet said, the "faithfulness" of many in these things is "like a morning cloud, and like the early dew it goes away" (Hos. 6:4).

When these things exist together, people feel hopeful that at least they are not under the dominion of sin. Nor is it easy to convince them that they are. And they may so conduct themselves in these things that it would be inconsistent with Christian charity to pronounce them so. Nevertheless, the fallacy in these things has been detected by many. And much more is required to give certain evidence of sincere faith and holiness. No one, therefore, can be acquitted from being subject to the reign of sin by pleading these things.

---

1. "Pleadable" means able to be offered as a formal plea in court.

CHAPTER 5

Sin Possessing the Imagination

We will now examine the second sort of signs from which arguments may be used to prove sin's dominion in a person but that are also inconclusive.

Two Observations

Before looking at these signs, we must observe two things.

First, that where sin has dominion it actually rules in the whole soul and its faculties. It is a depraved tendency in all the faculties, corrupting them in their various natures and powers, according to their capabilities:

- Sin thus produces darkness and vanity in the *mind*.
- Sin produces spiritual deceit and perverseness in the *will*.
- And it produces stubbornness and sensuality in the *heart*.

Sin in its power reaches and affects all the faculties of the soul.

Second, sin shows its dominion and is to be tested by its motions in the distinct faculties of the mind, the frame of the heart, and the direction and conduct of the life.

In examining the following signs, we will consider both those that render the case uncertain and those that clearly show sin's dominion. Therefore, I will not now give positive evidence of men's freedom from the dominion of sin but consider only the arguments that lie against them and examine how far they are conclusive or how they may be defeated.

A Dangerous Symptom

And first, any instance in which sin has possessed the imagination, thus engaging the cognitive faculty in its service, is a dangerous symptom of its rule or dominion. Sin may exercise its rule in the mind and imagination, where bodily strength or opportunity gives no advantage for its outward expression. In them the desires of sin may be as large as hell and the satisfaction of lust taken in with greed. Pride, covetousness, and sensuality may reign and rage in the mind through corrupt imaginations, though their outward expression is hindered by the circumstances of life.

The imagination is the first way in which sin acts. By this it turns its motions and inclinations into actions (Gen. 6:5). The continual evil figments of the heart are like the bubbling of corrupt waters from a corrupt fountain.

These imaginations consist in fixing the mind on

sinful objects by continuous thoughts with satisfaction and delight. This is how the mind makes provision for the satisfaction of the flesh and its lusts (Rom. 13:14), by which evil thoughts come to lodge, abide, and dwell in the heart (Jer. 4:14).

This is the primary and characteristic effect of that vanity of mind by which the soul is alienated from the life of God. The mind, being turned off with dislike from its proper object, applies itself by its thoughts and imaginations to the pleasures and advantages of sin. By this it seeks in vain to recover the rest and satisfaction lost through forsaking God Himself: "Those who regard worthless idols forsake their own Mercy" (Jonah 2:8). And when they surrender themselves with delight and approval to a constant inward association with the desires of the flesh and the pleasures and advantages of sin, then sin may reign triumphantly in them—even though they give no indication of it in the outward behavior. As the apostle declares, such have "a form of godliness but [deny] its power" (2 Tim. 3:5). Their hearts are filled with a brood of ungodly desires.

Three Examples

There are three evils in which sin especially exercises its reigning power in the imagination.

Pride, Self-Elation, Desire of Power and Greatness

It is affirmed of the prince of Tyre that he said, "I am a god, I sit in the seat of gods" (Ezek. 28:2); similar foolish thoughts are ascribed to the king of Babylon (Isa. 14:13–14). No matter how great the glory, power, and dominion in this world men can attain, they can yet in their imaginations and desires infinitely exceed what they enjoy—like the man who wept because he had no more worlds to conquer.[1] Such have no bounds; they want to be like God—indeed, to be God. This was the first design of sin in the world. And there is no one so poor and low but by his imaginations can lift up and exalt himself into the place of God. This vanity and madness God reproves in His discourse with Job (Job 40:9–14). And there is nothing more germane to and characteristic of the original depravation and corruption of our nature than this self-exaltation in foolish thoughts and imaginations. For this first came upon us through the desire to be like God. In this, therefore, sin exercises its dominion in the minds of men.

Indeed, the deceitful ways of sin primarily consist in the empty wind and vanity of these imaginations (and those that follow). The ways of men cannot satisfy themselves with the sins they actually commit but rove endlessly in these imaginations, finding satisfaction in their rejuvenation and variety (Isa. 57:10).

---

1. For Owen's thorough treatment of this sequence of temptation, see especially *The Nature, Deceit, and Prevalency of the Remainders of Indwelling Sin in Believers*, in *Works*, 6:153–322.

Sin Possessing the Imagination 41

Sensuality and Uncleanness of Life

It is said of some that they have "eyes full of adultery," and they "cannot cease from sin" (2 Peter 2:14). In other words, their imaginations are continually working about the objects of their unclean lusts. They think about these night and day, continually polluting themselves in all filth. Jude calls them "dreamers" who "defile the flesh" (Jude 8). By their vile imaginations, they live as if in a constant pleasing dream even when they cannot accomplish their lustful desires, for such imaginations cannot be better expressed than by dreams. Men satisfy themselves in this with an imaginary acting of what they don't do. By this many wallow in the mire of uncleanness all their days, with most never lacking in the effects of it when they have opportunity and advantage. By this means the most cloistered recluses may live in constant adulteries; by this, multitudes of them become sinkholes of uncleanness. It is this that, at its root, is severely condemned by our Savior (Matt. 5:28).

Unbelief, Distrust, and Hard Thoughts of God

These are of the same kind. Sometimes they will possess the imaginations of men so as to keep them away from all delight in God and to devise ways of fleeing from Him. But this is a peculiar case, not to be considered now.

In these and similar ways sin may exercise its dominion in the soul through the mind and its imagination. It may do this when no demonstration is made of it in outward behavior. By this the minds of men are defiled so that nothing is clean, all things are impure to them: "To the pure all things are pure, but to those who are defiled and unbelieving nothing is pure; but even their mind and conscience are defiled" (Titus 1:15). With their minds thus defiled, so are all things defiled to them: their enjoyments, their duties—indeed, all that they have and do.

Yet every failure and sin of this kind does not absolutely prove that sin has the dominion in the mind that it had before. Something of this vice and evil may be found in those who are freed from sin's reign—and this will be so until the vanity of our minds is perfectly cured and taken away. And this will not happen in this world. Therefore, I will name the exceptions that may be made against the title of sin to dominion in the soul, notwithstanding the continual work of the imagination in producing evil figments in the heart in some measure.

Four Exceptions

There are four exceptions to evil imaginations proving that one is absolutely under the dominion of sin.

Occasional Imaginations

Such imaginations are no evidence of sin's dominion when they are occasional, arising from the strength of some present temptation. As an example, take the case of David. In no way do I doubt that in his temptation and sin with Bathsheba, his mind was possessed with defiling imaginations. This is why, upon his repentance, he not only prayed for forgiveness of his sin but also cried

Sin Possessing the Imagination 43

fervently that God would "create in me a clean heart" (Ps. 51:10). He was conscious of his defilement not only of his person through actual adultery but also of his heart through impure imaginations. So it may be in the case of other temptations. As long as men are entangled with any temptation of whatever sort, it will multiply thoughts about it in the mind. Indeed, its whole power consists of a multiplication of evil imaginations. By these it blinds the mind, draws it away from considering its duty, and entices to the full conceiving of sin: "But each one is tempted when he is drawn away by his own desires and enticed. Then, when desire has conceived, it gives birth to sin; and sin, when it is full-grown, brings forth death" (James 1:14–15).[2] And so in this case of a strong temptation that may befall a true believer, the corrupt working of the imagination does not prove the dominion of sin.

If you ask how the mind may be freed from these perplexing, defiling imaginations that arise from the urgency of some present temptation (whether about worldly affairs or something similar), my answer is that it will never be done by the strictest watchfulness and resolution against them nor by the most resolute rejection of them. They will return with new violence and

---

2. For Owen's thorough treatment of this sequence of temptation, see especially *The Nature, Deceit, and Prevalency of the Remainders of Indwelling Sin in Believers*, in *Works*, 6:153–322.

new pretenses, though the soul has promised itself a thousand times that they should not do so.

There is only one way to cure this distemper, and this is by a thorough mortification[3] of the lust that feeds them and is fed by them. It is to no purpose in such cases to shake off the fruit unless we dig up the root. Every temptation designs the satisfaction of some lust of the flesh or the mind. These evil thoughts and imaginations are the work of temptation in the mind. There is no way to rid oneself from them, no conquest to be gained over them, except by subduing the temptation. And there is no subduing the temptation except through mortifying the lust that the temptation is designed to satisfy. The apostle directs us to this method:

> Set your mind on things above, not on things on the earth. For you died, and your life is hidden with Christ in God. When Christ who is our life appears, then you also will appear with Him in glory.
>
> Therefore put to death your members which are on the earth: fornication, uncleanness, passion,

---

3. "Mortification" refers to the Spirit-empowered process of putting sin to death, based on passages like Romans 8:13 and Colossians 3:5. For more on mortification in Owen, see book 4, chapter 8 in *Pneumatologia: A Discourse Concerning the Holy Spirit*, in *Works*, 3:538–65, and *Of the Mortification of Sin in Believers*, in *Works*, 6:1–86. For Owen's brief instruction in this book on how to mortify sin, see chapter 7.

Sin Possessing the Imagination

evil desire, and covetousness, which is idolatry. (Col. 3:2–5)

He commands us not to set our minds on things of the earth but rather on things above. In other words, we should not fill our imaginations and thus our affections with them. But how are we enabled to do this except by the universal mortification of sin (v. 5)?

Many people, because of a lack of wisdom and knowledge in this or for lack of practice through a secret unwillingness to fully mortify sin, are vexed and perplexed and, indeed, defiled, with foolish and vain imaginations all their days. Although this does not prove the dominion of sin, yet it deprives the soul of the peace and comfort it might otherwise enjoy.

Yet much spiritual skill and diligence are required to expose the true root and spring of the foolish imaginations that possess the mind. For they lie deep in the heart, and the heart is deep and deceitful. There are many other pretenses of them. They do not directly suggest the pride or unclean lusts from which they proceed but make other pretenses and feign other ends. But the soul that is watchful and diligent may trace them to their origins. And when such thoughts are strictly examined as to their design and whose work they do and what makes them so busy in the mind, they will confess the truth, both where they come from and what they aim at. Then the mind will be guided to its duty—namely, the extermination of the lust for which they make provision.

Afflictive to the Soul

Such imaginations, whatever their degree, are no evidence of sin's dominion when they are afflictive; that is, when they are a burden to the soul, which groans under them and would be delivered from them. The apostle gives a full account of this conflict between indwelling sin and grace in Romans 7. And the things he ascribes to sin are not the first risings or involuntary motions of it nor merely its inclinations and disposition. For the things ascribed to it, such as that it fights, rebels, wars, leads captive, acts as a law, cannot belong to them. Nor does he intend the outward acting or committing of sin—the doing, accomplishing, or finishing of it. For that cannot befall believers, as the apostle John declares in 1 John 3:9. He means rather the working of sin by these imaginations in the mind and the engagement of the affections. And this he declares to be the great burden of the souls of believers, what causes them to think their condition in some ways miserable and wretched. Because of this, they earnestly cry out for deliverance: "O wretched man that I am! Who will deliver me from this body of death?" (Rom. 7:24).

This is the case we have in mind. These figments of the heart, these imaginations arise in the minds of men, sometimes to a great degree. They are imposed on us with deceit and violence, leading us captive to their law. Where they are rejected, condemned, and defied they will return again, as long as there is any remaining vanity in the mind or corruption in the affections. But if the

Sin Possessing the Imagination

soul is conscious of them; if it labors under them; if it looks on them as enemies that fight against its purity, holiness, and peace; and if it prays for deliverance from them, then they are no argument for the dominion of sin. Indeed, the constant engagement of the mind in firm opposition to them is great evidence to the contrary.

A Strong Hatred of the Lust from Which They Proceed

Such imaginations are not proof of sin's dominion when a person maintains in their mind a strong hatred of the lust from which they proceed. Sometimes, I confess, this cannot be discerned. And all such varied imaginations are merely effects of the incurable vanity and instability of our minds, for these continually lead to random thoughts. But as we've already observed, they are usually employed in the service of some lust and tend toward its satisfaction. This is what the apostle forbids in Romans 13:14: "Make no provision for the flesh, to fulfill its lusts." And with strict examination, this may be discerned. And when the mind is fixed in constant hatred of the sin into which these imaginations lead, as it is sin against God, and when there is a firm resolution against this in all circumstances, no proof can be taken from these thoughts for the dominion of sin.

Injections of Satan

Sometimes evil thoughts are the immediate injections of Satan. On many accounts these are most terrible to the soul. For the matter of them is dreadful, often blasphemous, while the manner of their entrance into the mind is usually surprising, impetuous, and irresistible. Many have concluded from such thoughts that they are absolutely under the power of sin and Satan. But by certain rules and infallible signs, the source from which they proceed is discerned. When this is seen, all pretenses to the dominion of sin in them must disappear.

And this is the first case, which renders uncertain the question of whether or not sin has dominion in us.

CHAPTER 6

Dangerous Signs of Sin's Dominion

There are several other dangerous signs of sin's dominion.

Sin Reigning in the Affections

It is a dangerous sign of sin's dominion whenever it has a superior power in the affections. Indeed, the affections are the throne of sin, where it executes its power. But as I have handled this case of the affections at length in my discourse on spiritual-mindedness,[1] I will only briefly mention it here, giving just one rule by which to discern the dominion of sin in them.

This is certain: where sin has the superior power and is predominant in our affections, there it has dominion in the whole soul. The rule is given to us for this purpose (1 John 2:15). We are obligated to love the Lord our God with all our heart and with all our soul (Matt. 22:37). And therefore, if there is a predominant love for anything else

---

1. See Owen, *The Grace and Duty of Being Spiritually Minded*, in *Works*, 7:267–498.

within us in which we prefer something else to God, it must be from the strength of a principle of sin within us.

And this is so regarding all other affections. If we love anything more than God—as we do if we will not part with it for His sake, even if it is like a right eye or right hand; and if we take more satisfaction and delight in something else and cleave to it with our thoughts and minds more than we cleave to God—as men commonly do in their lusts, interests, enjoyments, and relationships; and if we trust it more than God for the provision of our needs—as most trust the world; and if we have stronger desires and greater diligence in seeking after and attaining other things than we do the love and favor of God; and if we fear the loss of other things more than we fear God—then we are not under the rule of God or His grace. We are under the dominion of sin, which reigns in our affections.

To give examples of this power of sin in and over the affections of men would be endless. Self-love, love for the world, delight in sensuality, placing too much value on relationships and pleasures, and many other things of a similar nature will easily show this.

And to resolve the case under consideration, we may observe two things. First, the strength of sin in the affections as a symptom of sin's dominion can be discerned by the least beam of spiritual light with a diligent searching into and judgment of ourselves. I do not know what can free people from sin's reign when they do not know and will not be convinced of sin. This is the case with many,

Dangerous Signs of Sin's Dominion

and we see it every day. There are people whose ways and deeds proclaim that they are driven in all things by an inordinate love for the world and self. Yet they find nothing amiss in themselves, and nothing in themselves to disapprove, except perhaps that their desires are not satisfied according to their expectations.

All the commands given in Scripture for testing ourselves, self-searching, and self-examination, and all rules that are given for examining ourselves, along with all the warnings given about the deceitfulness of sin and the deceitfulness of our own hearts, are given for this purpose: to prevent this evil of shutting our eyes against the strong corruption and disorder of our affections. The purpose of all our endeavors of this kind is seen in the appeal of David to God Himself in Psalm 139:23–24: "Search me, O God, and know my heart: try me, and know my thoughts: and see if there be any wicked way in me, and lead me in the way everlasting" (KJV).

Second, when people have convictions concerning the disorder of their affections yet are resolved to continue in their state without correction and change because of some advantage and satisfaction they receive in their present state, then they seem to be under sin's dominion. So it is with those mentioned in Isaiah 57:10:

> You are wearied in the length of your way;
> Yet you did not say, "There is no hope."
> You have found the life of your hand;
> Therefore you were not grieved.

They will not endeavor to change their corrupt affections because of the satisfaction, delight, and pleasure their affections take in inordinately cleaving to their objects.

This, then, is the only safe rule in this case: whatever hold sin may have over our affections, whatever strength it may have in them, and however it may entangle and defile them, if we sincerely endeavor to search out this evil and then constantly set ourselves to mortify our corrupt affections using all appropriate means, then there is not an argument in our disordered affections to prove sin's dominion in us. The proper objects of the great duty of mortification are our corrupt affections. That is why the apostle calls them our "members which are on the earth" (Col. 3:5).

This is a safe anchor for the soul in this storm: If it lives in a sincere endeavor to mortify every corruption and disorder we discern in the affections, then it is secure from the dominion of sin. But those who are negligent in searching into the state of their souls concerning the inclination and engagement of their affections and who approve of themselves in their greatest disorders must find their own pleas for vindication; I do not know any. But the meaning of this present rule will be further seen in what follows.

Neglecting the Duties for Mortifying Sin

It is another dangerous sign of sin's dominion when sin leads to neglecting the ways and duties that are most

Dangerous Signs of Sin's Dominion

suited and ordained for its mortification and destruction. When someone neglects these, especially after being convicted of their necessity, it is a dangerous sign.

The nature of mortification can be clarified by the following points:

- Mortification of sin is the constant duty of all believers who desire that sin not hold dominion over them. Where mortification is sincere, there is no dominion of sin. Where there is no mortification, there sin reigns.

- There are some graces and duties that are especially suited and ordained for this purpose. By them and their agency, the work of mortification can be constantly continued in their souls. We shall shortly consider what some of these are.[2]

- It is the duty of the soul to diligently apply these graces and duties that are specifically designed for mortification, especially when sin puts forth its power in any particular lust or strong inclination to any actual sin.

- It is a dangerous sign that sin has the dominion when men have been convicted of these duties and have attended to them according

---

2. See chapter 7, "Graces and Duties for Mortifying Sin," for Owen's further development of this point, as well as his book *Of the Mortification of Sin in Believers*, in *Works*, 6:1–86.

to that conviction, but then sin prevails in them to neglect and give up those duties or to give them up as it relates to their application to mortifying sin. I distinguish between these things—namely, a neglect of performing duties in general and a neglect of them for the purpose of mortifying sin. For men may continue to observe duties (or some of them) for other reasons yet not apply them to this specific purpose. And all external duties may continue to be observed when sin reigns in triumph (2 Tim. 3:5).

Holding On to Sin

Another sign of sin's dominion is holding on to any known sin against the light and power of convictions. We see this in the case of Naaman in 2 Kings 5. He would do anything, except for the one thing on which his honor and profit depended.

But where there is sincerity in conviction, it extends itself to all sins, for conviction is of sin as sin. One is thus equally convicted of every known sin—anything that has the nature of sin in it. And to be true to one's convictions is the essence of sincerity. If men can choose to make exceptions or hold on to certain sins in spite of being convinced of its evil, this is from sin's ruling power.

Prevalent pleas in the mind on behalf of any sin (that is, pleas for continuing in sin) ruin all sincerity. The pretense may be that it is just a little sin or one with no great consequence or one that will be compensated with other duties of obedience. Or maybe it will be held on to only until there is a better time for giving it up. Or having been convicted, men may later be blinded to dispute again whether it is actually sinful or not to tolerate it. This is frequently the case with covetousness, pride, and conformity to the world. It is a dreadful effect of sin's ruling power. Anything that challenges complete obedience in one thing overthrows sincerity in all things.

Hardness of Heart

Another evidence of sin's dominion is hardness of heart, which is frequently mentioned and complained of in the Scriptures. But because there are also various degrees of this, these must be considered in order to rightly judge when it is evidence of sin's dominion and when it might be consistent with the rule of grace. For it is a mysterious evil of which the best men most complain and in which the worst have no consciousness at all.[3]

---

3. See chapters 8 and 9 for Owen's further distinguishing between these different kinds and degrees of hardness of heart.

CHAPTER 7

Graces and Duties for Mortifying Sin

Having stated the meaning of the assertion that neglecting duties for mortifying sin is a dangerous symptom that sin holds dominion,[1] I will now consider some of the graces and duties for mortifying sin. When these duties are omitted or neglected, sin will prevail.

Faith in Christ Crucified
The first duty is the daily exercise of faith in Christ as crucified. This is the great fundamental means of the mortification of sin in general. And we should apply this to every particular instance of sin. The apostle speaks of this at length in Romans 6:6–13. He said, "Our old man was crucified with [Christ], that the body of sin might be done away with, that we should no longer be slaves of sin." Our "old man," or the body of sin, is the power and reign of sin in us. These are to be destroyed. They are so

---

1. That is, that neglecting duties for mortifying sin is a dangerous symptom that sin holds dominion. See third sign in chapter 6 above.

mortified "that we should no longer be slaves of sin"—we should be delivered from its power and rule. This, says the apostle, is done in Christ: "Our old man was crucified with Him" (v. 6).

This is true *meritoriously* in His actual dying or being crucified for us. This is true *virtually* because of the certain provision that was made in His death for the mortification of all sin. But this is also true *actually* by the exercise of faith in Christ as crucified, dead, and buried, which is the means by which the virtue of His death is communicated to us for that purpose. In this we are said to be dead and buried with Him. Baptism is the pledge of this. So by the cross of Christ the world is crucified to us, and we are crucified to the world (Gal. 6:14). This is the substance of the mortification of all sin.

There are several ways in which the exercise of faith in Christ crucified is effective for this purpose. First, looking to Him as crucified will cause holy mourning in us. "They will look on Me whom they pierced" and "will mourn" (Zech. 12:10). This is a promise of gospel times and gospel grace. The view of Christ as pierced will cause mourning in those who have received the promise of the Spirit of grace and supplication there mentioned by Zechariah. And this mourning is the foundation of mortification. It is the "godly sorrow [that] produces repentance leading to salvation, not to be regretted" (2 Cor. 7:10). And mortification of sin is of the essence of repentance.

Graces and Duties for Mortifying Sin 59

The more believers are exercised in this view of Christ, the humbler they are. And the more they will then be kept in the frame of mourning that is universally opposed to all the interests of sin and keeps the soul watchful against all its attempts. Sin never reigned in a humble, mourning soul.

Second, it is effective for this purpose by giving a powerful motive in calling and leading to conformity to Christ. This is pressed by the apostle in Romans 6:8–11. Our conformity to Christ as crucified and dead consists in our being dead to sin, thus overthrowing sin's reign in our mortal bodies. Paul says we ought to reckon this conformity as our duty: "Reckon yourselves to be dead indeed to sin" (Rom. 6:11). In other words, in aiming at conformity to Christ crucified, you should be truly dead to sin.

Can any spiritual eye behold Christ dying for sin and continue to live in sin? Shall we keep alive in our hearts those sins for which He died in order to keep them from eternally destroying us? Can we behold Him bleeding for our sins and not strive to give them their death wound? All believers know by experience how the exercise of faith in Christ crucified is effectual to mortifying sin.

Third, faith also gives us communion with Christ in His death, uniting our souls to the cross in its efficacy. This is why we are said to be "buried with Him through baptism into death" and "united together in the likeness of His death" (Rom. 6:4–5). Our "old man was crucified with Him" (v. 6). By faith we have communion with Him in His death, which leads to the death of sin.

This is, therefore, the first grace and duty we should attend to for the mortification of sin. But where sin has such interest and power in the mind that it takes the mind away from this exercise of faith—either by preventing or obstructing it so that the mind will not dare to think or meditate on Christ crucified because of the inconsistency of such thoughts with an indulgence to any sinful desire—it is to be feared that sin is on the throne.

If this is anyone's case and they have not yet made use of this means for mortifying sin, or, if being convicted of this, they have been driven away for a season from exercising faith in Christ crucified, my only advice for freeing them from this evidence of sin's dominion is for them to quickly and carefully apply themselves to this duty. Doing so successfully will bring its own evidence of freedom from sin.

It may be some will say that they are "unskilled" in this "word of righteousness," as some indeed are (Heb. 5:13). They do not know how to make use of Christ crucified for this purpose nor how to set themselves about it. They understand other ways of mortification. They are aware of the disciplines and penances assigned by Papists[2] for mortification. They understand vows and resolutions and other prescribed duties. But they understand nothing

---

2. *Papists* are Roman Catholics.

Graces and Duties for Mortifying Sin 61

about this way of deriving virtue from the death of Christ for the death of sin.

I can easily believe that some people would say this. In fact, they ought to if they were to truly speak their minds. For the spiritual wisdom of faith is required for true gospel mortification, but "not all have faith" (2 Thess. 3:2). Having lost this wisdom, the Papists have invented another way to replace this whole exercise of faith. They make crucifixes—images of Christ crucified—then adore, embrace, mourn over, and expect great virtue from them. Without these images they do not know how to seek Christ for the imparting of virtue from His death or life.

Others may be at the same loss, but they would do well to consider the reasons for this loss. For is it not from ignorance of the mystery of the gospel and the way in which the gospel imparts supplies of spiritual things from Christ? Is it not from ignorance of the power of His life and death for our sanctification and for mortifying sin? Indeed, is it not because they have never been thoroughly distressed in their minds and consciences by sin's power and thus have never earnestly sought for relief? Light, general convictions of either the guilt or power of sin will not drive anyone to Christ. But when their consciences are truly distressed so that they know not what to do, then they will learn how to "look" to Him "whom they pierced."

Those who do not find the daily necessity of applying themselves by faith to Christ for help and assistance are in a dangerous condition. Isn't this because they go to other reliefs? That's what their own promises and resolutions are. And these usually only serve to cheat and quiet the conscience for an hour or a day but then vanish to nothing.

Whatever the cause of this neglect, such people will pine away in their sins. For nothing but the death of Christ *for* us will be the death of sin *in* us.

Continual Prayer

Continual prayer is another duty that is necessary for mortifying sin. By this we are considering how to use prayer to fight against the particular desires in which sin especially exerts its power and seeks to control us. Continual prayer is God's great ordinance for sin's mortification.

This is true for several reasons. First, we obtain spiritual assistance and supplies of strength against sin by prayer. We should pray just as fervently that sin's power may be subdued as we pray that sin's guilt may be pardoned. He who neglects to pray against sin's power is not sincere in praying for its pardon, for the pressures and troubles we experience from sin's power are as sharp in the mind as the troubles caused by guilt in the conscience. Mere pardon of sin will never give peace to a soul. Although there is no peace without pardon, sin must also be mortified, or we can have no spiritual rest.

And this is the work of prayer: to seek and obtain such supplies of mortifying, sanctifying grace as will break

Graces and Duties for Mortifying Sin

sin's power, abate sin's strength, wither sin's root, and destroy sin's life, so that the whole old man is crucified. This is what the apostle prayed for the Thessalonians, and all believers should pray this daily for themselves: "Now may the God of peace Himself sanctify you completely; and may your whole spirit, soul, and body be preserved blameless at the coming of our Lord Jesus Christ" (1 Thess. 5:23).

Second, constant attention to the duty of prayer in an appropriate manner will preserve the soul in a condition in which sin cannot habitually prevail. He who can live in sin and abide in the ordinary duties of prayer never once prays as he should. If we simply go through the motions of worship or secretly hold on to sin, it spoils everything. A genuine, gracious, prayerful condition, in which we pray continually, is completely inconsistent with loving and holding on to sin. To pray well is to pray always—that is, to always keep the heart in the condition that is required in prayer. Where this is present, sin can have no rule or quiet harbor in the soul.

Third, the soul's immediate conflict against the power of sin is through prayer. Sin is the soul's enemy and fights against it. But in prayer the soul sets itself to grapple with sin, to wound, kill, and destroy it. Through prayer, the soul applies all its spiritual weapons to sin's utter ruin. Through prayer, the soul exercises a gracious hatred against sin and clear self-condemnation on account of sin. Prayer engages faith on all God's promises for sin's conquest and destruction.

This makes it evident that if sin has prevailed in someone's mind to cause them to neglect this duty, either in general or for its effective application against any sin that exerts its power, this is a dangerous symptom of sin's dominion in the soul.

It is certain that unmortified sin, any sin that is indulged, will gradually squeeze out all due regard to the duty of prayer. It will alienate the mind from either the matter of prayer itself or the manner in which we should pray. We see this exemplified every day in apostates. Though they once had a gift for prayer and were constant in the exercise of it, the love of sin and living in sin has devoured their gift and completely taken the duty of prayer off their minds. This is the true character of hypocrites. "Will he delight himself in the Almighty? Will he always call on God?" (Job 27:10). He may call on God for a season, but falling under the power of sin, he will not continue to do so.

Now, since sin uses great deceit in this gradual progress for achieving its purpose and thus securing its dominion, we should note some of its steps. This will serve to warn and caution us against sin so that we can fight its entrance. For just as "the entrance of [God's] words gives light" (Ps. 119:130)—that is, spiritual light to the mind—so the entrance of sin brings darkness, leading to a neglect of this duty. And just as the first motions of God's word on the mind should be improved, so the first motions of sin on the mind should be fought.

Step 1: Sin Produces an Unreadiness in the Mind to Pray

Sin produces in the mind an unreadiness to engage in the duty of prayer in its appointed seasons. The heart should always rejoice in the approach of these seasons because in them it has delight in God. To rejoice and be glad in all our approaches to God is always required of us. Therefore, as we think about and approach these seasons, we should groan within for a mind so prepared that it will fit us for the communion with God to which we are called. But when sin begins to prevail, things will be unprepared and out of order. A strange reluctance will rise in the mind toward either the duty of praying itself or the appropriate manner of praying. One will be tempted to just go through the motions of prayer. The body seems to carry the mind to the duty of prayer, whether the mind is ready or not, rather than the mind leading the body. And the mind will concern itself with anything rather than attending to the duty at hand.

A great part of our wisdom in avoiding the power of sin in us thus lies in this: that we continually keep our hearts in a gracious disposition and readiness for prayer in all its appropriate seasons. If you lose ground here, you will keep going further backward. Know, therefore, that there is no more effective way of preserving the soul against sin's power than a gracious readiness for and disposition to this duty of prayer in both private and public, according to their appropriate seasons.

Step 2: Sin Produces an Unwillingness to Pray

Sin in its progress will add to unreadiness in the mind and unwillingness in the heart, for the mind that is consumed with sin finds prayer directly opposed to its present interests and inclinations. For there is nothing in prayer that does not trouble and disquiet the interests of sin. Just as the king of Israel who was not willing to hear the prophet because "he does not prophesy good concerning me, but evil" (1 Kings 22:8), so sin causes a secret unwillingness to prevail in the mind, a dislike of any serious engagement in prayer. When such people do attend to prayer, it is as if they were forced to do so in order to comply with customs or convictions.

Step 3: Sin Leads to Total Neglect of Prayer

Sin will eventually lead to total neglect of the duty of prayer. This observation is confirmed by long experience. If prayer does not strive constantly to ruin sin, then sin will ruin prayer and completely alienate the soul from it. This is the way of backsliders in heart. As they grow in sin, they decay in prayer until they are weary of it and completely give it up. So they say, "Oh, what a weariness!" (Mal. 1:13). They look at prayer as a task and a burden and are weary attending to it.

In saying this neglect of the duty of prayer is an effect of sin's dominion, I do not mean that people give up prayer completely or absolutely, so that they completely abandon all ways of prayer, whether public or private, or completely forsake all seasons and occasions of prayer. Few people rise to such shamelessness in sin, to such desperate opposition to God. They may still attend to the stated seasons of prayer in families or in public assemblies. They may draw near to God with their lips. And in times of danger, they will personally cry out to God, as Scripture everywhere testifies of them. In saying they neglect this duty, I mean only this: that they no longer apply prayer to the mortification and ruin of the lust or corruption in which sin exercises its power and rule in them in a sincere, prompt, and direct way. And where this is so, sin seems to have the dominion. Of such a person the psalmist said,

> He has ceased to be wise and to do good.
> He devises wickedness on his bed;
> He sets himself in a way that is not good;
> He does not abhor evil. (Ps. 36:3–4)

What I'm speaking of is a habitual neglect of the duty of prayer for this purpose of mortifying sin that leaves the soul with a false sense of security. For it is possible for this evil, through the power of temptation, to temporarily overcome believers. God thus complains of His people, "You have not called upon Me, O Jacob; and you have been weary of Me, O Israel" (Isa. 43:22). In other words, compared to the fervency and sincerity required of them, they were weary of calling on God.

But when believers are temporarily in this condition through the power of sin and temptation, they do not approve of themselves. They will now and then call things to consideration and say, "It is not with us as it should be or as it was in former days. This thing is not good that we do, nor will it be peace in the latter end." Also, in this condition they will have secret resolutions of shaking themselves out of the dust of this evil state. They say in themselves, "I will go and return to my first husband, for then it was better for me than now" (Hos. 2:7). When they are in this condition, they will look on everything that befalls them in a way of mercy or affliction as calls from God to deliver them and recover them from their backslidden condition. Also, they will receive the warnings that are given to them through the preached word, especially if their particular case is touched or exposed. Finally, they will have no quiet or rest and will not approve of themselves until they are thoroughly healed and recovered (see Hos. 14:1–4).

Therefore, it is possible that this will befall some people who are not under sin's dominion. Yet they should diligently watch against the first entrance of sin as something that leads to the danger and ruin of the soul.

Constant Humility

Another duty that is directly opposed to the interest and rule of sin in the soul is constant self-abasement, condemnation, and hatred of sin. No frame of mind is a better antidote against sin's poison. He who walks humbly walks securely (see Prov. 10:9). God has a continual regard for mourners, those who are of a "broken spirit…and a contrite heart" (Ps. 51:17). This is the soil in which all grace will thrive and flourish. A constant due sense of sin as sin and of how this concerns us by nature and in the course of our lives, with an ongoing and afflicting remembering of our particular sins, leading to a gracious self-abasement, is the soul's best posture in watching against all the deceits and attacks of sin.

We should attend to this duty with all diligence. We are wise to keep our souls in a constant attitude of mourning and self-abasement, with reference to all the purposes of the life of God. Far from being inconsistent with the consolations and joys offered by the gospel to us in believing, this is the only way to truly let them into the soul. To such mourners, and them alone, are evangelical comforts given:

> I have seen his ways, and will heal him;
> I will also lead him,
> And restore comforts to him
> And to his mourners. (Isa. 57:18)

One of the first things sin does in aiming for dominion is to destroy this frame of mind. And when it actually has the rule, it will not allow it to enter. Sin makes men careless and unconcerned about this. Indeed, it makes them bold, presumptuous, and fearless. Sin blocks the self-reflections and considerations that lead to this frame from entering the mind. It represents them as either needless or untimely. It makes the mind afraid of them as things that lead to distress and have no benefit. If sin prevails in this, it makes way for the security of its own dominion.

Nothing is more watched against by those who are under the rule of grace than a proud, heedless, foolish frame of heart.

CHAPTER 8

Two Kinds of Hardness of Heart

Hardness of heart can be either total and absolute or partial and only relative.[1]

Total Hardness of Heart

Total hardness can be either natural and universal or judicial in some particular individuals. *Natural hardness* is the blindness or obstinance of the heart in sin by nature. This cannot be cured by the use or application of any outward means; Paul speaks of their "hardness and…impenitent heart" (Rom. 2:5). This is the heart of stone, which, in the covenant, God promises to take away by the power of His almighty grace (Ezek. 36:26). Where this hardness remains uncured and unremoved, there sin is absolutely on the throne. This is not the kind of hardness now under consideration.

---

1. The next two chapters on hardness of heart are Owen's further development of the fifth dangerous sign of sin's dominion (see chapter 6).

Judicial hardness comes either immediately from God or through the devil by God's permission. First, it can come directly from God, who is frequently said to harden the hearts of men in their sins, leading to their ruin, as in the case of Pharaoh (Ex. 4:21). Generally, He does this in two ways: first, by withholding from them those supplies of light, wisdom, and understanding, without which they cannot understand their condition, see their danger, or avoid their ruin; second, by withholding the effectual power of the means to which they do have access—indeed, He gives them an efficacy leading to their hardening (Isa. 6:9–10).

There are several things we may observe concerning this divine process of hardening: It is the most severe divine punishment that takes place in this world. Therefore, it is only executed toward those who are habitually wicked, who by their own choice harden themselves in their sins (Rom. 1:26, 28). It usually concerns particular times and seasons that are turning points for eternity. The condition of those who are hardened in this way is without remedy; their wounds are incurable. When any are hardened in this way, there is no question but that they are under the dominion of sin. Such a heart is sin's throne, its proper seat, next only to hell.

There is also a judicial hardness that Satan, through God's permission, brings upon men: Their "minds the god of this age has blinded, who do not believe, lest the light of the gospel of the glory of Christ, who is the image of God, should shine on them" (2 Cor. 4:4). There are many ways by which Satan effects this hardening, but these are not to be considered here.

Partial Hardness of Heart

But there is also a hardness of heart that is only partial and relative, even though it may appear to be total and absolute. This is why we must inquire whether or not hardness of heart is evidence of sin's dominion.

There is a kind of hardness of heart that is known and lamented by those who have it. The church complains of this in Isaiah 63:17: "O LORD, why have You made us stray from Your ways, and hardened our heart from Your fear?" Or, as the sense may be, Why have You suffered it to be so, rather than healing and recovering us from our hardness? And there are various things that work together in this kind of hardness of heart.

The Heart Lacks Readiness to Receive God's Word

When the heart is soft and tender, it is also humble and contrite and ready to tremble at God's word. So it was said of Josiah that his heart was tender and he humbled himself before the Lord when he heard His word (2 Kings 22:18–19).

But this readiness can be lacking in great measure, and people may be conscious of it. They may find within themselves a great unreadiness to comply with divine warnings, reproofs, and calls. They are not affected by the preached word but sometimes complain that they sit under it like stocks and stones. They do not have an experience of its power and are not cast in its mold. And in this they realize that their hearts are hardened from fearing God, as the church complains. There is, indeed, no better frame of heart to be attained in this life than when the heart is like wax to the seal—soft and tender, ready to receive the communications of God's word in all their variety, whether reproof, instruction, or consolation. The lack of this readiness is a culpable hardness of heart.

The Heart Lacks Sorrow and Repentance for Sin
No one who possesses a spark of saving grace lacks a gracious sorrow for sin to some degree or another. But there is a proportion required between sin and sorrow. Great sins require great sorrows. Peter, after his great sin, "wept bitterly" (Luke 22:62). And all special aggravations of sin require a special sense of them. The soul does not find this within itself. It bears the thoughts of sin and the rebukes of conscience without any great sense of grief or remorse. It passes over the charge of sin without relenting, mourning, or dissolving into sighs and tears. Such a heart is sometimes as hard as a rock.

This causes many to fear that they are under the dominion of sin. And they fear it more because their fear does not affect and humble them as it should. And it must be granted that any lack of being affected with sin and any lack of humiliation and godly sorrow come from an undue hardness of heart. Such people have a great reason to be watchful over themselves and concerned for their spiritual state and condition.

The Heart Is Unaffected by the Sins of Others

To mourn for the sins of others is a duty highly approved of by God (Ezek. 9:4). Such mourning indicates the effectual work of many graces, such as zeal for God's glory, compassion for the souls of men, and love for the glory and name of Christ in the world. The lack of this comes from hardness of heart and abounds among us. Some people find themselves completely unconcerned about this. Others make excuses for their lack or argue that it is not their duty—for what is the world's wickedness to them? Let it answer for its own sins!

Nor are such people moved when it strikes closer to home. If their children come to loss, poverty, and ruin, then they will be affected. But as long as they flourish in the world, they are not very concerned (especially if they are not scandalously profligate)—even if their children are apostates from their profession of faith or live as enemies to Christ and walk as those who openly belong to the world. But this also is from hardness of heart. And this will be lamented where grace is vigilant and active.

The Heart Lacks Awareness of the Signs of God's Displeasure

God often gives signs and tokens of His displeasure, whether regarding the public state of the church in the world or our own persons. He does this in afflictions and chastening. In such seasons He expects our hearts to be soft and tender, ready to receive impressions of His displeasure and thus become pliable to His mind and will. And there are none He abhors more at such times than those who are stouthearted and show little regard for Him or for the work of His hands. This may be in believers in some measure. And they may be sensible of this, leading to their sorrow and humiliation.

These things and many more of a similar nature proceed from hardness of heart or the remnants of our natural hardness. These things greatly promote the interests of sin in us.

But when people are conscious of this frame, are humbled for it, mourn under it, and cry out for its removal, then, far from being evidence of sin's dominion, it is rather an eminent sign of the contrary—namely, that the ruling power of sin is certainly broken and destroyed in the soul.

CHAPTER 9

Diagnosing the Dominion of Sin

There are other cases of hardness of heart that have much more difficulty in them. And these are more difficult to reconcile with the rule of grace.

Dangerous but Not Indisputable Signs

The following cases are dangerous, though not indisputable, signs of sin's dominion.

Security and Apathy Under the Guilt of Great Sins

I do not say that this can be absolute in any believer. But there are cases in which men may go on with their former duties and profession of faith while under the provoking guilt of some known sin with all its aggravations—yet without any deep humiliation for their sin. Though guilt recurs on their mind and conscience (unless it is seared) and troubles them, they pass it over as something they would rather forget instead of rightly dealing with the sin through specific repentance.

This seems to have been the case with David after his sin with Bathsheba. Before he heard the message of God sent to him through Nathan, he doubtless had unpleasant thoughts about what he had done. But there are not the least indications in the story or in any of his prayers to suggest that he had seriously laid it to heart or was humbled (see 2 Sam. 11). This was a great hardness of heart, and we know how difficult his recovery from it was. He was saved, but as through fire.

And when this is the case with anyone who has been overtaken with any great sin, such as drunkenness or some other folly, and they strive to pass over it, forget it, or find it acceptable to avoid consideration and humiliation for it, then they cannot in that state of mind have solid evidence that sin does not have the dominion in them. Those sinners who have passed over former sins till they have lost all sense of them or are now in such a hardened frame of mind should be warned to bring themselves to account and not allow such sin to pass without humiliation. If they do not do this, they have no solid ground for spiritual peace in this world, whatever may be their final outcome.

The Guilt of One Sin Does Not Make the Soul Watchful Against Others

When a tender heart is overtaken by a temptation into sin, it will not only watch against returning temptation and future relapses into that sin but will become diligent, heedful, and careful against all other kinds of sins. So it is with all who walk humbly when conscious of sin.

But when men are in a careless, bold, and negligent state, then even if they do not repeat the same sin, they are easily hurried into others. This was the case with Asa. When a prophet came to him with a divine message, he was "angry with the seer, and put him in prison" (2 Chron. 16:10). One would think that when he had recovered from this distemper, it would have made him humble and watchful against other sins. But it was not so, for it is added that he "oppressed some of the people at that time" (v. 10). And he didn't rest in this, but "in his disease he did not seek the LORD, but the physicians" (v. 12). To persecution he added oppression, and to that unbelief. Notwithstanding all this, "Asa's heart was loyal to the LORD all his days" (1 Kings 15:14). That is, he had a dominant sincerity within him, notwithstanding these failures. But he was doubtless under the power of great hardness of heart.

So it is with others in similar cases when one sin makes them not careful and watchful against another. For example, when men have stained themselves with intemperance of life, they may fall into excessive anger with their families and relations or into a neglect of duty or take other crooked steps in their walk. This argues a great strength of sin in the soul, although (as we see in the example of Asa) it is not infallible evidence of its dominion. Yet divine peace and consolation are inconsistent with the nature of it.

Ordinary Means of Grace Do Not Bring Recovery

Men can fall into unspiritual conditions, such as spiritual deadness and decay, and the ordinary means of grace will not recover them. This is strong evidence of hardness of heart and the strength of sin in it. This is so, whether it is the fault of churches or of individuals. The preaching of the word is the special divine ordinance for the healing and recovery of backsliders in heart and life. Where this will not bring recovery in someone but instead they stubbornly go on in the ways of their own hearts, they are on the brink of ruin unless God takes some extraordinary measures with them. They live on sovereign grace alone.

It was like this with David. After his great sin, he doubtless attended all the ordinances of divine worship, which are the ordinary means of the preservation and recovery of sinners from their backslidings. But they didn't have this effect on him. He continued to live impenitently in his sin, until God was pleased to use extraordinary means for his awakening and recovery—namely, the message of Nathan and the death of his child (see 2 Sam. 12).

And God will thus sometimes deal with churches and people. Where ordinary means for their recovery will not work, He will heal, revive, and save them by sovereign grace and perhaps by a concurrence of extraordinary providences. He promises to do just this (Isa. 57:16–19). But when people depend on God's sovereign grace and extraordinary providences while neglecting the ordinary means of healing, the end may be bitterness and sorrow since there is no direct promise of this; this is, rather, a case reserved to absolute sovereignty. Let those who think this way, therefore, take heed. For although God may deliver them, yet it will be by terrible things (see Ps. 65:5)—such terrible things as those in which he "took vengeance on their deeds" (Ps. 99:8), even though He forgives them. So David says of himself that in dealing with him, God had broken all his bones (Ps. 51:8).

I fear this is the present case of many churches and professing Christians today. It is obvious that they have fallen under many spiritual decays. Nor have the ordinary means of grace, repentance, and humiliation been effective to bring about their recovery—though backed with various providential warnings. It is greatly to be feared that God will use some severe dispensation in terrible things toward them for their awakening or withdraw His presence from them, which is even more dreadful.

An Unfruitful Profession of Faith

When men satisfy and please themselves in an unmortified, unfruitful profession of faith, this also argues no small power of this evil. This is a severe symptom of sin's dominion. There are three things that show how this is a fruit of hardness of heart.

The first is a neglect of primary duties, such as mortification of sin in oneself and usefulness or fruitfulness toward others. Many who profess religion are deficient and neglectful of these things. Nothing indicates that they seriously strive for mortification of their lusts, pride, passion, love for the world, inordinate desires, or sensual appetites. They either indulge them all or at least fail to maintain constant warfare against them. And they are completely barren when it comes to usefulness in the fruits of righteousness, or good works. Such fruits are to the praise of God by Jesus Christ, while good works are the evidence of a living faith. But though they profess religion, they neglect these primary commands of it. Their deficiency in these comes from hardness of heart, which overpowers their light and convictions. In such a case, what will long keep sin off the throne? Self-pleasing and satisfaction in such a state indicates a very dangerous condition and frame of mind. Sin may have full dominion in such a profession.

Second, and similarly, is accepting habitual formality in the performance of religious duties. As I observed before, sin's power prevails in some people to the neglect and omission of such duties. Others continue to observe them but in such a formal and lifeless way with such lack of concern to exercise grace in their duties that it gives uncontrollable evidence of sin's power and spiritual insensibility in the heart.

The Scriptures condemn nothing more frequently and severely than diligent attendance to and multiplication of duties while the heart is not spiritually engaged in them. This is characteristic of hypocrites. This was the reason the Lord Christ threatened to completely reject the lukewarm church of Laodicea. And God pronounces a most severe sentence against all who are so guilty (Isa. 29:13–14).

Yet this is the condition of many and has been the case of many who manifest their open apostasy, which is the common outcome of continuing long in this condition and way of life. Certain people will exercise and preserve their gifts in some daily performance of religious duties for a season. But since there is no exercise of grace in them, their gifts also wither and decay. When people can approve of themselves in such a lifeless, heartless profession of religion and performance of duties, they are under this power of evil we are considering—namely, a hard and senseless heart.

Third is when people grow insensible under the ministry of the word and derive no profit from it. The general purposes of preaching the word to believers are these:

- the increase of spiritual light, knowledge, and understanding in them;

- the growth of grace, which enables obedience;

- the holy stirring up of grace by impressions of its power in communicating the mind, will, love, and grace of God to our souls, which is accompanied by an impression on the affections, renewing and making continually more holy and heavenly;

- the direction and administration of spiritual strength against temptations and corruptions; and

- fruitfulness in the works and duties of obedience.

But when people can continue under the ministry of the word without any of these effects on their minds, consciences, or lives, they are greatly hardened by the deceitfulness of sin. This case is stated in Hebrews 3:12–13.

Whether this is from the carelessness and security that develops in all sorts of people and against which God justly expresses His indignation by withholding the power and efficacy of His word in its ministry; or from an increase of unsanctified light and gifts that fill people with high thoughts of themselves and keep them from a humble, teachable frame of mind; or from a loss of all due reverence to the ministry as God's ordinance for all the stated purposes of His word, with a secret fortification of the conscience, against its power, from the suggestions of Satan; or from the love of sin, which the heart attempts to shelter and secure from the power of the word—or from any other cause—this proceeds from a dangerous hardness of heart and the power of sin.

When this is the state of people's minds and this hardness is dominant in them, no one can give them assurance that sin does not have the dominion in them.

Diagnosing the Dominion of Sin

Because all these things can be present in various degrees, however, sin's dominion over someone cannot be absolutely concluded from any degree of any or all of them.

But we may safely conclude the following: that unless he strives against it, it is impossible for anyone in whom this evil frame is found in any degree to keep a true and solid peace with God or his own soul. Such a condition appears to be ruinous; this is the high road to final hardness and impenitence. Therefore, it is the present duty of those who have any care in their souls to shake themselves out of this dust. They should give themselves no rest until they have entered into the paths of recovery. God's calls to return to such backsliders in heart are multiplied, and the reasons and motives for them are without number. This should never depart from their minds, for without it they will eternally perish. And they do not know how soon they may be overtaken with destruction.

We have thus considered whether sin has dominion in us or not. On the other hand, there are many evidences of the rule of grace that are sufficient to discard the pleas and pretenses of sin to the throne. But it has not been my purpose to consider them.[1] I have only examined the pleas made by sin that make discernment difficult and the case uncertain. These all arise from the motions of sin within us as it fights against the soul, for this is its constant and characteristic work (1 Peter 2:11).

---

1. But see the next section, "Indisputable Signs of Sin's Dominion."

Sin thus works against the design of the law, which is to live to God; against the order and peace of the soul, which it disturbs; and against the soul's eternal blessedness, which sin would deprive the soul from receiving. And this examination may be useful to some who are sincere.

Indisputable Signs of Sin's Dominion

But on the other hand, there are indisputable signs of sin's dominion in men, which I will only mention because they do not need proof or illustration. Sin has dominion

- when it has possessed the will. And it has possessed the will when there are no restraints from sinning taken from the nature of sin, but only from its consequences.

- when people proclaim their sins and do not hide them—when they boast in them and about them, as is the case with multitudes of people.

- when people approve of themselves in any known sin (such as drunkenness, uncleanness, swearing, and similar sins) without repentance.

- when people live in neglect of religious duties in their closets and families. In this case, all public attendance to duties is just hypocrisy.

- when people are at enmity to true holiness and the power of godliness.

Diagnosing the Dominion of Sin

- when people are visible apostates from their profession of faith, especially if they add to their apostasy persecution—as they usually do.
- when people are ignorant of the sanctifying principles of the gospel.
- when people despise the means of conversion.
- when people live in security under open providential warnings and calls to repentance.
- when people are enemies in their minds to the true interest of Christ in the world.

Where these and similar things are found, there is no question about it: sin has dominion and bears rule in the minds of men. All people can easily know this, as the apostle declares in Romans 6:16.

PART 3

The Assurance of Freedom from Sin's Dominion

What is the reason for the assurance here given to us that sin will not have dominion over us—namely, because we are "not under law but under grace"?

CHAPTER 10

Sin's Dominion over Those Under the Law

I have now written much concerning the second thing proposed at the beginning of this book—namely, how we may know whether or not sin has dominion in us. I now proceed to the third question: What is the assurance given to us that sin will not have dominion over us? And what is the reason for this assurance? The answer lies in this: that we are "not under law but under grace" (Rom. 6:14).

Where men are engaged in a constant conflict against sin; where they look on sin and judge it their greatest enemy, which fights for their souls and their eternal ruin; where they have experienced sin's power and deceit and through these have often been shaken in their peace and comfort; where they have been ready to despond and say they will one day perish under sin's power, then it is a gospel word, a message of good news, that gives them assurance sin will never have dominion over them.

The ground of this assurance is this: that believers are "not under the law, but under grace." And I will show the force of this reason in several things.

The Law Gives No Strength

First, the law gives no strength against sin to those who are under it, but grace does. Sin will not be either cast out or kept off its throne unless there is a spiritual power and strength in the soul to oppose, conquer, and dethrone it. Where sin is not conquered, it will reign. And it will not be conquered without a mighty, triumphant power. This the law will not and cannot give.

The law must be taken in two ways. First, the law can refer to the whole revelation of God's mind and will in the Old Testament. In this sense the law had grace in it and gave life, light, and strength against sin, as the psalmist declares (Ps. 19:7–9). In this sense, it contained not only the law of precepts but also the promise and the covenant. And this was the means of conveying spiritual life and strength to the church. But this is not the sense in which the law is spoken of here, nor is the law in this sense anywhere opposed to grace.

The second way the law must be taken is as a covenant rule of perfect obedience: "Do this and live."[1] In this sense men are said to be "under the law" in opposition to being "under grace." They are under its power, rule, conditions, and authority as a covenant.

---

1. See Galatians 3:12, which quotes Leviticus 18:5.

And in this sense all men are under it who are not instated in the new covenant through faith in Jesus Christ, who sets up in them and over them the rule of grace. For all people are under the rule of God in one way or the other, and He rules only by the law or by grace. And no one can be under both at the same time.

The Purpose of the Law

The law, in this sense, was never ordained by God to convey grace or spiritual strength to the souls of men. Had it been so, the promise and gospel would have been unnecessary. "If there had been a law given which could have given life, truly righteousness would have been by the law" (Gal. 3:21). If the law could have given life or strength, it would have produced righteousness, and we could have been justified by it. The law exposes sin and condemns it, but it does not give strength to oppose sin. It is not God's ordinance for dethroning sin or destroying its dominion.

This law falls under a twofold consideration. But in neither of these was it designed to give power or strength against sin.

First, the law must be considered as it was given to mankind in the state of innocence. The law then declared the whole duty of man absolutely and exactly, showing what God in His wisdom and holiness requires of us. This was God's rule over humanity according to the principle of the righteousness in which we were created. But the law gave no new help against sin, nor was there need for it to. It was not God's ordinance to administer new or more grace to people but to rule and govern them according to what they had received. And it continued to do this forever. The law claims and continues as an authority over all people, according to what they had and have. But it never had power to block the entrance of sin or to cast it out once enthroned.

Second, the law must be considered as it was renewed and commanded to the church of Israel on Mount Sinai. The law was given to Israel and to all out of the nations of the world who would join themselves to the Lord. Yet it was not then designed for the purpose of destroying or dethroning sin through the administration of strength and grace.

The law, then, did have some new purposes given to it that it did not have in its original constitution. The primary one was to drive people to the promise and to Christ in the promise. It does this by all its works and powers on the souls of men. The law drives us to this end as it exposes sin, as it irritates and provokes sin by its severity, as it judges and condemns sin, and as it pronounces a curse on sinners. These purposes were graciously added in the renewal of it. But in itself, the law had nothing to do with sinners except to judge, curse, and condemn them.

Therefore, we can expect no help from the law against sin's dominion. It was never ordained by God for this purpose, nor does it contain or communicate grace necessary for that end: "For what the law could not do in that it was weak through the flesh, God did by sending His own Son in the likeness of sinful flesh, on account of sin: He condemned sin in the flesh" (Rom. 8:3).

Sin's Dominion Through the Law

For this reason, those who are under the law are under the dominion of sin. "The law is holy," but it cannot make holy those who have made themselves unholy. The law is "just," but it cannot make people just; it cannot justify those whom it condemns. The law is "good," but it can do them no good as it concerns their deliverance from the power of sin (see Rom. 7:12–13). God has not appointed it for this purpose. Sin will never be dethroned by it. Sin will not give place to the law, neither in its title nor its power.

Those who are under the law, however, sometimes attempt to shake off the yoke of sin, resolving to live under its power no longer. They do this, for example, when the law presses their consciences, perplexing and disturbing them. The commandment comes home to them, sin revives, and they die (Rom. 7:9–11). In other words, the law gives sin power to slay the hopes of the sinner and to distress him with the fear of guilt and death. For "the strength of sin is the law" (1 Cor. 15:56)—its power to disturb and condemn sinners is in and by the law. When this is the case with sinners—when the law presses them with a sense of sin's guilt and deprives them of all rest and peace in their minds—they will resolve to cast off the yoke of sin and to relinquish its service, that they might be freed from the urgency of the law on their consciences. They will strive to do this in instances of duty and abstinence from sin.

People do the same thing when surprised with sickness, pain, dangers, or death itself. Then they will cry and pray and promise to reform and set about it, as they suppose, with sincerity. This case is fully illustrated in Psalm 78:34–37, and it is seen in daily experience among multitudes of people. Few people are so seared and shameless that they will not in such seasons think about returning to God, relinquishing the service of sin, and vindicating themselves from under its dominion. In some it works a lasting change, even though there is no real conversion. But with most people, their "faithfulness is like a morning cloud, and like the early dew it goes away" (Hos. 6:4).

The same effect is produced in many by the preaching of the word. Some arrow of conviction is fastened in their minds, and so their former ways displease them. They judge that it would be better to change the way of their lives and to relinquish the service of sin. But these resolutions usually stay with them according to the society they have or fall into. Good society may greatly help them in their resolve for a while. But evil and corrupt society eventually extinguish their resolve.

Sometimes merciful, endearing providences have the same effect on the minds of those who are not hardened

Sin's Dominion over Those Under the Law

in sin. Examples of this would be deliverances from imminent danger, when a family member's life is spared, and other similar situations. People under the law in such seasons will pay attention to their convictions and temporarily strive to shake off the yoke of sin. They will listen to the law (under whose power they are) and what it says. And they will strive to comply with it. They will perform many duties and abstain from many evils in order to quit themselves of sin's dominion. But, alas, the law cannot help them with this. It cannot give them life or strength to go through with what their convictions press them to do. Therefore, after a while they begin to faint and grow weary in their progress and eventually give up. Perhaps they break off some specific great sins, but they cannot shake off sin's whole dominion.

CHAPTER 11

Grace Gives Strength Against Sin

The situation is different for those who are under grace. Sin will not have dominion over them. They are given strength to dethrone sin.

Liberation from Sin's Dominion

Grace is a word with various connotations in Scripture. Here, where it is said that we are under grace as opposed to the law, the word is used or taken for the gospel. For the gospel is God's instrument for communicating Himself and His grace by Jesus Christ to those who believe, along with the state of acceptance with God, into which the gospel brings them. Romans 5:1–2 says, "Therefore, having been justified by faith, we have peace with God through our Lord Jesus Christ, through whom also we have access by faith into this grace in which we stand, and rejoice in hope of the glory of God." To be under grace is thus to have an interest in the gospel covenant and state, with a right to all its privileges and benefits.

It is to be brought under the administration of grace by Jesus Christ. It is to be a true believer.

But the inquiry here is this: Why does being under grace mean that sin will not have dominion over us? Why can sin not extend its territories and rule into the state of those under grace? And in what sense is this affirmed?

Does it mean that there is no longer any sin within them? Even this is true in some sense. For sin in regard to its condemning power has no place in this state: "There is therefore now no condemnation to those who are in Christ Jesus, who do not walk according to the flesh, but according to the Spirit" (Rom. 8:1). All the sins of those who believe are expiated in the blood of Christ. Their guilt is done away (Heb. 1:3; 1 John 1:7). This branch of sin's dominion, consisting in its condemning power, is utterly cast out of this state.

Ongoing Conflict with Sin

But in regard to its existence and operation, sin continues to work in believers as long as they are in this world. All believers are conscious of this. Those who deceive themselves with a contrary understanding are most of all under the power of sin: "If we say that we have no sin, we deceive ourselves, and the truth is not in us" (1 John 1:8).

This is why to be freed from sin's dominion does not mean that we are absolutely freed from all sin, so that it should no longer dwell within us in any sense. That is not to be under grace but to be in glory.

Grace Gives Strength Against Sin

Does it mean that sin, though it dwells within, no longer fights or contends for dominion in us? This is contrary to what we've already seen. Scripture and the common experience of all who believe testify to the opposite. In fact, the assurance given here that sin shall not obtain dominion confirms this. For if it did not contend for dominion, there could be no grace in this promise. For there is no grace in deliverance from that of which we are in no danger.

The assurance given to us here is built on other considerations. The first is that the gospel is the ordained means and instrument that God uses for the communication of spiritual strength to those who believe, for the dethroning of sin. For the gospel "is the power of God to salvation" (Rom. 1:16). It is that by and in which God puts forth His power for this purpose. And sin really must be dethroned by the powerful work of grace within us.

And this involves us in the way of duty. By the promise of the gospel, we are absolved and freed from the rule of sin, its usurped right and title. For by this we are discharged from the rule of the law, in which sin's title to dominion is founded—for "the strength of sin is the law" (1 Cor. 15:56).

But we are freed from sin in its internal power and the exercise of its dominion by internal spiritual grace and strength in its due exercise. And this is communicated by the gospel. The gospel gives us life and power, with the continual supplies of grace that can dethrone sin and forever prohibit its return.

This then is the case being considered by the apostle: "You who are believers are all engaged in conflict with sin. You find it always restless and disturbing and sometimes strong and powerful. When it is joined with an urgent temptation, you fear that it will completely triumph over you, to the ruin of your souls. So you are wearied with it, groan under it, and cry out for deliverance from it." The apostle generally insists on all these things in Romans 6 and 7. "But now," he says, "be of comfort. Notwithstanding all these things and your fears because of them, sin will not prevail. It will not have dominion. It will never ruin your souls."

But what ground do we have for this hope? What is our assurance for this success?

"This you have," says the apostle. "You are not under law but under grace"—that is, the rule of God's grace in Christ Jesus administered in the gospel.

But how does this give relief? The apostle answers, "Because it is the ordinance and instrument of God, which He will use for this purpose—namely, to give you such supplies of grace and spiritual strength as shall eternally defeat sin's dominion."

The Difference Between Law and Gospel

This is one principal difference between the law and the gospel (and was ever so esteemed in the church of

Grace Gives Strength Against Sin

God, until all communication of effectual grace began to be called in question): the law guides, directs, and commands all things that are against the interest and rule of sin. It judges and condemns both the things that promote it and the people who do them. It frightens and terrifies the consciences of those who are under its dominion. But if you say to the law, "What then should we do? This tyrant, this enemy, is too hard for us. What aid and assistance will you offer us? What power will you give us for its destruction?" Here the law is completely silent. Or it says that nothing like this is committed to it by God. No, whatever strength the law has, it gives to sin, for the condemnation of the sinner: "The strength of sin is the law" (1 Cor. 15:56).

But the gospel (or the grace of the gospel) is God's means and instrument for communicating internal spiritual strength to believers. By the gospel they receive supplies of the Spirit and the assistance of grace for the subduing of sin and the destruction of its dominion. By the gospel they can do all things through Him who enables them.

On this, then, depends the apostle's assurance that sin will not have dominion over us—because we are under grace. This is the first ground of assurance for this assertion. We are in a state in which we have ready supplies to defeat all the attempts of sin for rule and dominion in us.

CHAPTER 12

Advice for Those Perplexed with Sin

But upon this, some may say that they greatly fear they are not in this state of grace, for they do not find such supplies of spiritual strength and grace as give them conquest over sin. They are still perplexed with sin. It is ready to invade the throne of their minds—if the mind is not possessed of sin already. For this reason, they fear that they are strangers to the grace of the gospel. In answer to this, I put forward the following.

Remember the Nature of Sin's Dominion

Remember what has already been declared concerning sin's dominion. If the dominion of sin (what it is and consists in) is not understood, some people may comfort themselves though their condition is dreadful (as do most), while others may be perplexed in their minds without just cause. Making a clear distinction between the *rebellion* of sin and the *dominion* of sin is a great advantage to spiritual peace.

Consider the Purpose of Gospel Helps

Consider the purpose for which helps to grace are granted and communicated by the gospel. These are given not that sin may be at once completely destroyed in us—that is, should no longer have any existence, activity, or power in us at all. That is reserved for glory, in the full redemption of body and soul, which we now only groan after.

The helps to grace are rather given to us for this purpose: sin may be so crucified and mortified in us (that is, so gradually weakened and destroyed) that it will not ruin spiritual life within us. They are given so that sin will not obstruct the necessary work of spiritual life in our duties and to give us strength against such sins as would break the covenant relationship between God and our souls.

As long as we have supplies of grace sufficient to this end, we are under grace, even though our conflict with sin continues and we are perplexed by it. But in this case, sin will no longer have dominion over us. And this is enough for us: that sin will gradually be destroyed, and we will have sufficient grace at all times to prevent its power to rule.

Expect to Receive Supplies of Grace

Live in the faith of this sacred truth and always keep alive in your souls the expectation of receiving supplies of grace that will meet this need. To believe that the gospel is God's way of administering grace for the ruin of

Advice for Those Perplexed with Sin

sin is in the nature of true, saving faith. It is inseparable from it.

He who does not believe this does not believe the gospel itself, which "is the power of God to salvation" (Rom. 1:16). If we live, walk, and act as if we have nothing to trust in but ourselves and our own efforts and resolutions during our perplexities and temptations, then it is no wonder that we are not conscious of supplies of divine grace. This probably means we are under the law, not grace.

This is a basic principle of the gospel state: that we live in expectation of receiving continual supplies of life, grace, and strength from Jesus Christ, "who is our life" (Col. 3:4) and from whose "fullness we have all received, and grace for grace" (John 1:16).

In this case we should therefore continually admonish our souls as David did:

> Why do I go mourning because
> of the oppression of the enemy?...
> Why are you cast down, O my soul?
> And why are you disquieted within me?
> Hope in God;
> For I shall yet praise Him,
> The help of my countenance and my God.
> (Ps. 42:9, 11)

We may be conscious of great oppression from the power of this enemy. This may cause us to mourn all day long—and in some sense it should. We should not despond in this, however, or be cast down from our duty or comfort. We may still trust in God through Christ and live in continual expectation of such spiritual reliefs as shall surely preserve us from sin's dominion.

The gospel calls us to this faith, hope, and expectation. And when this expectation is not cherished and maintained in order to be rightly exercised, everything in our spiritual condition will go backward.

Ask the Lord for Grace

Go to the Lord Christ for special supplies of grace. The administration of all spiritual supplies is committed to Him so that He can give them to you, according to your need in all situations.

Does sin have the advantage of a powerful temptation, so that it seems to struggle for dominion in the soul? As the Lord answered Paul's repeated prayer when he was buffeted by Satan, "My grace is sufficient for you" (2 Cor. 12:9). Sin will not have dominion over you.

Has sin, by its deceit, brought your soul into a lifeless, senseless frame? Has it made your soul forgetful of duties, negligent in them, or without spiritual delight in them? Has it made your soul almost accustomed to careless and corrupt inclinations and to love for and conformity to the world? Does it take advantage of darkness and confusion in the face of troubles, distresses, and temptations? In these and in all similar situations, it is required that we go fervently to the Lord Christ for such supplies of grace as will be sufficient and effectual to control the power of sin. We are directed to do this as we consider His office and authority for this purpose, along with His grace and readiness to help in special need (Heb. 4:14–16).

Remember How Grace Works

Always remember the way and method by which divine grace and spiritual supplies work. It is true that in our first conversion to God, we are (as it were) surprised by a mighty act of sovereign grace that changes our hearts, renews our minds, and quickens us with a principle of spiritual life.

Ordinarily, many things are required of us in the way of duty to prepare for this. There are many previous operations of grace in our minds that materially and passively dispose us to this in illumination and conviction of sin—just as dry wood is disposed to catch fire. But the work itself is done by an immediate act of divine power without any active cooperation on our part.

But this is not the law or rule by which actual grace is communicated and operates for the subduing of sin. This grace is given in a way of concurrence with us in the discharge of our duties. And when we are diligent in them, we may be sure that we will not fail to receive divine assistance, according to the established method by which gospel grace is administered.

Therefore, if we complain that we do not find the supplies mentioned but at the same time are not diligent in attending to all the duties by which sin may be mortified in us, then we are exceedingly injurious to God's grace.

Therefore, despite this objection, since spiritual supplies are administered by grace for the mortification and destruction of sin, the truth stands firm, that "sin shall not have dominion over [us], for [we] are not under law but under grace" (Rom. 6:14).

CHAPTER 13

Freedom Through the Gospel

The law gives no liberty of any kind. It produces bondage and thus cannot free us from dominion. It cannot liberate us from sin. But this is what we have through the gospel, for the gospel gives us a twofold liberty or freedom: a liberty in our state or condition and an internal freedom in the soul.

Freedom from the Curse of the Law

The first aspect of liberty consists in our deliverance from the law and its curse, with all its claims against us. This includes Satan, death, and hell. We could never be delivered from this state by the law. But by grace we are transferred into a state of glorious freedom, for by it the Son makes us free and we receive the Spirit of Christ. And "where the Spirit of the Lord is, there is liberty" (2 Cor. 3:17).

Christ proclaims this liberty in the gospel to all who believe. As he says in Isaiah 61:1:

> The Spirit of the Lord GOD is upon Me,
> Because the LORD has anointed Me
> To preach good tidings to the poor;
> He has sent Me to heal the brokenhearted,
> To proclaim liberty to the captives,

And the opening of the prison to those who are bound.

Then those who hear and receive the joyful news are discharged from all debts, bonds, accounts, rights, and titles and are brought into a state of perfect freedom. In this state sin can lay no claim to dominion over any one soul. They have departed from the power of sin, Satan, and darkness and have crossed over into the kingdom of Christ.

Indeed, the foundation of our assured freedom from sin's rule lies in this. Sin cannot make an inroad into Christ's kingdom so as to carry any of His subjects back into a state of sin and darkness. Therefore, our interest in this state should be pleaded against all the attempts of sin against us (Rom. 6:1–2).

Nothing should be more hated than for one of Christ's free people who is now dead to the power of sin to surrender ground to any of sin's pretenses or attempts to rule.

Freedom in the Mind and Heart

There is also internal liberty, freedom of the mind and heart from the powerful inward chains of sin. This freedom gives an ability to exercise all the powers and faculties of the soul in a gracious manner. By this the power of sin in the soul is destroyed.

And this is also given to us in the gospel. For through the gospel, power is given to live to God and walk in His commands. This also shows the truth of the apostle's assertion: "Sin shall not have dominion over you, for you are not under law but under grace" (Rom. 6:14).

Freedom from Fear

The law does not supply us with effectual motives and encouragements to attempt the ruin of sin's dominion in a way of duty. But we must ruin sin's dominion, or it will prevail in the end. The law, however, works only by fear and dread, with threats and terrors of destruction. For although it says, "Do this and live," yet it also exposes the inability in our nature to comply with its commands in the way and manner required. Thus, the very promise of life through obedience becomes a matter of terror, for it also includes the opposite: the sentence of death for the failure to obey its commands.

These things then enervate, weaken, and discourage the soul in its conflict against sin. They give no life, activity, cheerfulness, or courage in what it undertakes. That is why those who have only the motives of the law quickly faint and give up when they engage themselves in opposition to sin or try to quit its service.

We see this with many every day. One day they will forsake all sin, even their beloved sin, along with the companions and occasions that lead them into sin. The law has frightened them with divine vengeance. And sometimes they go so far in this resolution that they seem to have escaped from the pollution of the world. Yet they soon return again to the former ways and follies (2 Peter 2:20–22). Their "faithfulness is like a morning cloud, and like the early dew it goes away" (Hos. 6:4).

Or if they do not return to wallow in the same mire of their former pollution, they embrace the shadows of superstitious observances, as seen in the papacy. For they openly follow the pattern of the Jews, who, "being ignorant of God's righteousness, and seeking to establish their own righteousness, have not submitted to the righteousness of God" (Rom. 10:3). For in that apostate church, people are worked on by the terrors of the law to relinquish sin and set themselves against its power. But in finding themselves altogether unable to do this by the works of the law, which requires perfect holiness, they embrace superstitious observances, trusting them instead of the law with its commands and duties. But the law makes nothing perfect, nor are its motives for the ruin of sin's interest in us able to bear us out and carry us through in that undertaking.

But grace gives us motives and encouragement to labor for the complete ruin of sin. These motives and encouragement give life, cheerfulness, courage, and perseverance. They continually animate, relieve, and revive the soul in all its work and duty. They keep us from fainting and despondency, for they are all taken from the love of God and Christ, the whole work and purpose of His mediation, the ready help of the Holy Spirit, all the promises of the gospel, and their own and other believers' experiences. All these give them the greatest assurance of final success and victory.

When someone is under the influence of these motives, no matter what difficulty or opposition they meet with from soliciting temptations, they, according to the promise of Isaiah 40:31,

> shall renew their strength....
> They shall run and not be weary,
> They shall walk and not faint.

Freedom in Christ

Freedom comes through the gospel of Christ, not through the law. Christ is not in the law.[1] He is not proposed in it, nor communicated by it, nor are we made partakers of Him by the law.

This is the work of grace, of the gospel. For in the gospel, Christ is revealed; by it He is proposed and

---

1. Remember that Owen is not speaking of the law in the broad sense, as comprising the full revelation of the Old Testament, but in the narrow sense, as "the covenant rule of perfect obedience," which says, "Do this and live." See chapter 10.

exhibited to us, and by it we are made partakers of Him and all the benefits of His mediation.

And it is Christ alone who came and was able to destroy this work of the devil: the dominion of sin. For sin's dominion is the accomplice to the devil's works, where all his designs center. And this is what "the Son of God was manifested, that He might destroy" (1 John 3:8). Christ alone ruins the kingdom of Satan, whose power is exercised in the rule of sin.

This, then, is how our assurance of this comforting truth is primarily resolved. For what Christ has done and continues to do for this purpose is one of the main points of gospel revelation.

And the same can be said concerning the gift of the Holy Spirit, who is the only principal efficient cause of the ruin of sin's dominion. For "where the Spirit of the Lord is, there is liberty" (2 Cor. 3:17)—and nowhere else. But we receive this Spirit not "by the works of the law," but "by the hearing of faith" (Gal. 3:2).

CHAPTER 14

The Mercy of Deliverance from Sin's Dominion

It is an unspeakable mercy and privilege to be delivered from the dominion of sin. The apostle declares this to be a privilege here in Romans 6, and those who believe esteem it so.

Nothing is more sweet, precious, and valuable to a soul in conflict with sin and temptation than to hear that sin will not have dominion over it. What would some give for this to be spoken to them with power, that they might believe it steadfastly and know its comfort? "Fools mock at sin" (Prov. 14:9), and some glory in serving sin. This is their shame. But those who understand anything in the right way, either what is present or what is to come, know that this freedom from sin's dominion is an invaluable mercy. Consider some of the reasons that show this to be so.

The Causes of This Freedom

It appears in the various causes of this mercy. Freedom from sin's dominion is something that no one can attain by their own power or the utmost of their endeavors. People by their endeavors can get rich or become educated or wise. But no one can by this means shake off the yoke of sin. If someone had all the wealth in the world, they could not purchase this freedom. It would be despised. And when sinners go from this world to the place where the rich man was tormented and have nothing more to do with this world, they would give all, if they could, for an interest in this freedom.

This freedom is something that the law and all its duties cannot acquire. As we've already seen, the law and its duties can never destroy sin's dominion. All people who ever come under the power of real conviction will discover this. When sin presses them and they are afraid of consequences, they find that the law is weak and the flesh is weak—and so are their duties, resolutions, and vows. None of these are able to bring them relief. And if they think themselves free one day, they find themselves again in bondage the next day. Despite all their efforts, sin will rule over them with force and rigor. And in this condition, some spend all their days in this world. Though they kindle sparks of their own making and walk in their light, they lie down in darkness and sorrow (Isa. 50:11). For they sin and promise to change and try to make up for sin with their duties, but they are never able to deliver themselves from the yoke of sin.

We can see the excellence of this privilege from its causes, of which I will mention only several.

The Meritorious Cause: The Death of Christ

This is what purchases our freedom. This is declared in 1 Peter 1:18–19; 1 Corinthians 6:20; and 1 Corinthians 7:23. Nothing else could purchase this freedom.

We were under the power and dominion of sin and could not be delivered without a ransom. "For to this end Christ died and rose and lived again, that He might be Lord of both the dead and the living" (Rom. 14:9) and thus deliver us from the power of all other lords. It is true that there was no ransom due to sin or Satan, the author of sin. They were to be dethroned and destroyed by an act of power. Both the devil and sin, which is his work, are to be destroyed, not appeased (Heb. 2:14; 1 John 3:8). But "the strength of sin is the law" (1 Cor. 15:56). This means that through the righteous sentence of God, we were held in our desperate condition under the condemning power of sin. And the only way we could be delivered from the law was through the payment of this ransom. From this, two things follow.

First, those who live in sin, who willingly continue in serving sin and endure its dominion, cast the greatest contempt on the wisdom, love, and grace of Christ. They despise that which cost Him so dearly. They judge the purchase of this freedom with His precious blood to have been very foolish. They prefer the present satisfaction of their lusts over freedom. This is the poison of unbelief, in which there is great contempt for the wisdom and love of Christ. The language of the hearts of men who live in sin is that this blood-bought freedom is not valuable. They flatter Him with their lips in the outward observance of some duties, but in their hearts, they despise Him and the whole work of His mediation. But the time is approaching when they will learn the difference between the slavery of sin and the freedom with which Christ makes believers free. And it is this freedom that is now offered to sinners in the ministry of the gospel. Life and death are here set before you. Choose life, that you may live forever.

Second, let those who are believers, in all their conflicts with sin, live in the exercise of faith in this purchase of freedom made by Christ's blood. For two things will follow from this. First, this will always give them a weighty argument, ready for opposing the deceit and violence of sin. The soul will say to itself, "Shall I forego and part with what Christ purchased for me at so costly a price by giving place to the solicitations of lust or sin? Shall I despise His purchase? God forbid!" (see Rom. 6:1–2). Through such arguments the mind is frequently kept from giving in to the enticements and seductions of sin.

Second, this is also an effective argument for faith to use in its pleading for deliverance from sin's power. We ask for nothing except what Christ has already purchased for us. And if this plea is pursued, it will be done.

The Internal Efficient Cause: The Holy Spirit

This is how the power and rule of sin are destroyed within us and a further demonstration of this mercy.

Every act for the mortification of sin is from the Spirit, as are the positive graces by which we are sanctified. For it is "by the Spirit" that we "put to death the deeds of the body" (Rom. 8:13). Where He is, there and there alone, is liberty. All attempts to mortify sin without His special help and operations are ineffective.

This is manifest in the extent of sin's dominion in the world. For people generally despise the Spirit by whom alone sin can be destroyed and all the effectual operations of the Spirit by which this is so. Such people must live and die as slaves to sin.

This is why a great part of our wisdom for attaining and keeping this liberty consists in acting faith on the promise of our Savior, that our heavenly Father will "give the Holy Spirit to those who ask Him!" (Luke 11:13). We are too ready to turn to ourselves and our own resolutions on any occasion when sin through temptation strives for power and rule in us. In their place, these are not to be neglected. But we shall find our best relief in immediately crying to God for such supplies of His Spirit, without which sin will not be subdued. Bear this in mind and try it the next time you are tempted. God will bless it with success.

The Instrumental Cause: The Duty of Believers

The instrumental cause of this freedom is the duty of believers themselves in and for the destruction of sin. This also shows the importance of this privilege. For one of the primary purposes of all our religious duties—whether prayer, fasting, meditation, or watchfulness to all other duties of obedience—is to ruin the interest of sin in us.

We are called into an arena to fight and contend, into a field to be tested in battle. Our enemy is sin, which strives and contends for the rule over us. We must resist this even to blood. And certainly, that which by divine appointment and command is the great purpose for the constant endeavors of our whole lives is of the greatest importance.

The Bondage from Which We Are Freed

This great mercy is also seen when we consider the bondage from which it delivers us. Human nature is most opposed to bondage until it is debased and debauched by sensual lusts. Throughout all ages, honest men have chosen to die rather than be made slaves. But there is no bondage like the dominion of sin. The worst slavery is to be under the power of degraded lusts such as covetousness, uncleanness, drunkenness, ambition, pride, and the like and to make provision to fulfill their desires in the will of the mind and the flesh.

But say what we please on this subject, none think themselves freer and none make such a show of giving freedom to others as those who are the open servants of sin. If those who do whatever they want and usually are approved in their actions, who scoff at all their enemies and scorn such fearful slaves who won't join them in the same excess are not free, then who is? Like the Pharisees, they say they are the only ones who are truly free and have never been in bondage to any (see John 8:33). They wholly despise the servile restraints of fear from divine judgment and future reckoning. See the description of this in Psalm 73:4–11. Who are as free and joyous as such persons, even while others are plagued all day long and "chastened every morning" (Ps. 73:14)? Indeed, they mourn under the oppression of this enemy, continually crying out for deliverance.

But the truth we insist on is not at all overthrown by this observation. For a great part of the slavery of such people is that they don't know they are slaves and boast that they are free. They are born into a state of enmity against God and bondage under sin. And they think it normal. Like abject slaves under the worst of tyrants, they don't know anything better. But true liberty consists in inward peace, tranquility of mind, intentions and inclinations toward the best things—the most noble objects of our rational souls. Those who spend their lives as slaves to vile and base lusts are strangers to all these things. Do not envy their brashness, their glittering appearance, or their heaps of wealth and treasure. On the whole, they are vile and contemptible slaves. The apostle judges their case in Romans 6:17: "But God be thanked that though you were slaves of sin, yet you obeyed from the heart that form of doctrine to which you were delivered." It is a matter of eternal thankfulness to God that we are delivered from being the "slaves of sin."

Indeed, when a soul is made really conscious of the excellence of this freedom and finds the power and interest of sin so weakened that it can rejoice and thank God for it, this is an evidence of grace and of a good frame of spirit (Rom. 7:25).

The Results of Bondage to Sin

The greatness of this mercy is seen in respect to the final result of this bondage, or what it brings men to. If they could expect anything like a future reward hereafter, following all the base drudgery to which sinful men are put in serving their lusts and all the conflicts they experience in their consciences with their fears and terrors in the world, then perhaps something could be said to alleviate their present misery. But "the wages of sin is death" (Rom. 6:23), eternal death under the wrath of the great God. This is all they have to look forward to. The end of sin's dominion is to give them over to the curse of the law and the power of the devil forever.

We see the greatness of this mercy when we consider how sin's dominion keeps people from participating in anything really good both here and hereafter. What people under the power of sin do enjoy will quickly appear to be "a thing of nought."[1]

And in the meantime, they do not have the least taste of God's love, which is the only thing that takes the

---

1. This is a frequently used phrase in the King James Version of the Bible. See Isaiah 29:21; 41:12; Jeremiah 14:14; and Amos 6:13.

poison out of our enjoyments. They do not have the least view of Christ's glory, without which they live in perpetual darkness, like those who never see the light of the sun. They have no experience of the sweet, excellent, and gracious life-giving influences of the Holy Spirit, of His strength and comfort, or of the satisfaction and reward found in holy obedience. And they shall never come to the enjoyment of God.

They have not the least view of the glory of Christ, without which they live in perpetual darkness, like those who never behold the light or sun. They have no experience of the sweetness and excellence of the gracious influences of life, strength, and comfort from the Holy Ghost; nor of the satisfaction and reward that is in holy obedience; nor will ever come to the enjoyment of God.

All these things and many more of the same kind could be insisted on and expounded on to show the greatness of the mercy and privilege found in freedom from dominion of sin, as here proposed by the apostle. But since I've accomplished the primary design I intended, I only touch on these things.

CHAPTER 15

Be Sure You Are Not Under Sin's Dominion

It is the great interest of a soul in conflict with the power of sin to secure itself against sin's dominion. Be certain that you are not under sin's rule. Do not leave this unsettled in the mind. To clarify this truth, we can observe the following things.

Continual Conflict with Sin
Remember that conflict with sin will continue as long as we are in this world. This makes continual repentance and mortification absolutely necessary. The pretense of perfection in this is contrary to the Scriptures and the common experience of all believers. It is also contrary to the sense and conscience of those who claim perfection, as they daily make evident.

We pray against sin, strive against sin, and groan for deliverance from sin. And by the grace of Christ healing our nature, this is not without success. But this success does not reach the absolute eradication of sin while we are in this world. Sin will abide in us until the union of soul and body is dissolved, for it is in this union that sin has incorporated itself. This is our lot and portion. This is the result of our departure from God and the resulting corruption of our nature.

Relief Through the Gospel

You will say, then, "What is the purpose of the gospel and the grace of our Lord Jesus Christ in this case, if it is not able to give us deliverance?" I answer, it gives us a fourfold relief that amounts to constant deliverance, even though sin remains in us as long as we are in this world.

The Continuance of Sin Within Us

It is so ordered that the continuance of sin within us shall be the ground, reason, and occasion for the exercise of all grace and of putting a luster on our obedience. Some excellent graces, such as repentance and mortification, could have no exercise if it were otherwise. But while we are in this world, there is a beauty in these graces that counterbalances for the evil of remaining sin.

The difficulty of obedience occasioned by remaining sin, thus continually calling for the exercise and use of all grace, makes it more valuable. In this lies the spring of humility and self-resignation of the will to God. This makes us love and long for the enjoyment of Christ and puts an excellency on His mediation. This is why, in consideration of this, the apostle exclaims, "I thank God—through Jesus Christ our Lord!" (Rom. 7:25). This makes our future rest and reward sweeter to our souls.

For this reason, our continuance in this state and condition of spiritual warfare in this world is best for us and greatly suited to divine wisdom, considering the office and care of our Lord Jesus Christ for our relief. Let us not complain, repine, or faint but instead go on with Christian fortitude to the end, and we shall have success.

Spiritual Strength Granted

Furthermore, by the grace of Christ there are such supplies and aids of spiritual strength granted to believers that sin will never proceed further in them than is useful and needful for the exercise of their graces. As we have already declared, sin will never have its will on them nor dominion over them.

Mercy in the Gospel

There is also mercy given in and through the gospel for the pardon of all that is evil—either in itself or in any of its effects. "There is therefore now no condemnation to those who are in Christ Jesus" (Rom. 8:1). Pardoning mercy, according to the tenor of the covenant, always disarms the condemning power of sin in believers. Thus, in spite of sin's greatest attempts, believers "having been justified by faith...have peace with God" (Rom. 5:1).

Sin Will Be Abolished

By the grace of Christ, there is a season when sin will be completely abolished. This will be at death when the course of our obedience is finished. For this reason, to affirm that sin (and consequently, conflict with sin) continues to dwell in believers while they are in the world is no disparagement to the grace of Christ. For it is grace that gives a blessed deliverance from sin.

Conflict with Sin Under the Reign of Grace

There is a double conflict with and against sin. There is first a conflict in those who are unregenerate. This consists in the rebellion of light and conscience against the rule of sin in particular situations. For although sin is enthroned in the will and affections, yet the knowledge of good and evil in the mind, excited by the hopes and fears of things eternal, will fight against it. This leads to the performance of many duties and abstinence from sin. But this conflict can exist where sin is on the throne. And people may deceive themselves in this, thinking that it is from the rule of grace, when it is only from the rebellion of light and the charge of a conscience not yet seared.

But there is another kind of conflict with sin in those in whom grace has the rule and is enthroned. For although grace rules in the mind and heart, yet the remainders of sin will be continually rebelling against it, especially in corrupt affections.

This means that it is in the interest of all to examine which kind of conflict with sin is going on within them. If it is the first kind, they may yet be under the dominion of sin. If it is of the second kind, then they are freed from it.

Be Sure You Are Not Under Sin's Dominion

For this reason, as long as the mind is uncertain and doubtful in this case, it will be perplexed with many evil consequences, such as these:

- Such a soul can have no solid peace because it is not certain which state it is in.

- It cannot be refreshed by gospel consolations because its just fears of sin's dominion will defeat them all.

- Without spiritual courage and delight, it will be dead and formal in all its duties. This will eventually make the soul weary of duties.

- Therefore, all grace, and especially faith, will continually be weakened and impaired under this frame.

- The fear of death will hold the soul in bondage.

This is why it is so important to have this case clearly understood and rightly determined in our minds. This book was written with this design in view.

CHAPTER 16

Directions to Prevent Sin's Dominion

Finally, I will give several directions for how the strength and dominance of sin may be removed or prevented to such a degree as to make the question of its rule doubtful in the mind. Many directions could be given, but I will propose the following ones.

Watch Against Sin's Beginning

The great rule for preventing the increase and power of vicious habits is to watch against beginnings. The way sin attempts to gain dominion is through particular instances, through one particular lust or another. This is why when any sin or corrupt lust begins to build up special strength or interest in the mind and affections, if not met with severe mortification, it will ruin the peace, if not endanger the safety of the soul.

Anyone who keeps a diligent watch over their heart may easily see when this is so. For no sin advances itself in the mind and affections without being supported by men's natural inclinations, circumstances, some temptation which they have exposed themselves to, or some such neglect in which the frequency of acts has strengthened evil inclinations. But these things can be easily discerned by those who are in any measure awakened to the concerns of their souls.

Our Lord Jesus Christ has given us a strict charge to "watch" (Matt. 26:41). And the wise man said that above all keepings we should keep our heart (see Prov. 4:23). These commands have special regard to the beginnings of sin's gaining power in us. If sin is not opposed with severe and diligent mortification, as soon as we discover how it has used any of these ways to increase its power, then it will continue in the method declared in James 1:14–15: "But each one is tempted when he is drawn away by his own desires and enticed. Then, when desire has conceived, it gives birth to sin; and sin, when it is full-grown, brings forth death."

Those who would be wise must train themselves in wisdom by an ongoing and open engagement with it. They must say to wisdom, "You are my sister," and call understanding their kinswoman (Prov. 7:4). Then wisdom will have power in and over their minds. But if we allow sin to grow familiar in our minds by any of the advantages mentioned, and if upon its first appearance of activity for power in us we do not say to it, "Get away from me," then it will press hard for the throne.

Examine Yourself

Carefully examine yourself to know whether you do or approve of anything in your life that promotes the power of sin, assisting its rule in your life. This is the method David prescribes in Psalm 19:12–13:

> Who can understand his errors?
> Cleanse me from secret faults.
> Keep back Your servant also from
>   presumptuous sins;
> Let them not have dominion over me.
> Then I shall be blameless,
> And I shall be innocent of great transgression.

"Secret faults," are things that we may not even know to be sins. These make way for those sins that are "presumptuous."

For example, pride might seem like nothing but a frame of mind belonging to our wealth, status, or abilities. Sensuality may seem like nothing but lawful participation in the good things of this life. Anger and irritability may appear to be due regard for the lack of respect that we think is due to us. And covetousness may seem like necessary care for us and our families. But if the seeds of sin are covered with such pretenses, they will eventually spring up and bear bitter fruit in people's minds and lives.

The beginnings of all apostasy, in both religion and morality, lie in such pretenses. People plead that they do such and such things lawfully but eventually do things that are openly unlawful.

Keep Your Heart Tender

Always keep your hearts tender under the word. This is the true and only state that is inconsistent with and opposed to the rule of sin. The loss of this tenderness, or a decay in it, has opened the floodgates of sin among us. But a conscientious fear of sinning will always prevail in the soul where this frame of mind is present. When it is lost, people will be bold in all sorts of follies.

That this frame may be preserved, several things are required:

- That we cast out all vicious habits of mind that are contrary to it (James 1:21).

- That we keep an experience of its power and efficacy in our souls (1 Peter 2:1–3).

- That we lay aside all prejudices against those who minister the word (Gal. 4:16).

- That we keep the heart always humble, for this is the only frame in which it is teachable (Ps. 25:9). For everything in the preaching of the word is cross and unpleasing to the minds of proud men.

- That we pray for blessing on the ministry of the word. This is the best preparation for receiving benefit from it.

Directions to Prevent Sin's Dominion 137

Abhor Peace with Compromise

Abhor the peace of mind that is consistent with any known sin. People may be frequently attacked and fall into known sins, but while this is so with them, if they refuse all inward peace, except that which comes by fervent and sincere desires for deliverance and repentance from sin, then they may be safe from sin's dominion.

But if they can (through hopes or presumptions or resolutions) preserve a kind of peace while living in any known sin, they are near the borders of carnal security. And this is the territory over which sin reigns.

Seek the Help of Christ

Make continual applications to the Lord Christ in all the acts of His mediation for the ruin of sin. Do this especially when it attempts to gain dominion in you (Heb. 4:16).

This is the life and soul of all the directions in this case and doesn't need to be expanded on. It is spoken to frequently.

Remember Your Deliverance

Finally, remember that a due sense of deliverance from sin's dominion is the most effective motive to complete obedience and holiness. And this is what the apostle proposes in Romans 6.